D0268294

AFRAID OF THE DARK

Ralph Riegel is the southern correspondent for Independent Newspapers and covers the region for the *Irish Independent*, *Sunday Independent* and *Evening Herald*. He has also reported for the INM group from the US, UK, Europe and Australia. He is a regular contributor to RTÉ, BBC1 (NI), *The Independent* and *The Daily Telegraph*. He has previously worked with papers including *The Avondhu*, *The Nationalist*, the *Waterford News & Star* and the *Irish Examiner* as well as magazines including *Irish Crime*. He also covered the Ian Bailey libel case for the updated edition of *Death in December* published by the O'Brien Press.

Leabharlann Shráid Chaoimhín
Kevin Street Library
Tel: 01 222 8488

AFRAID OF the DARK

The Tragic Story of Robert Holohan

Ralph Riegel

THE O'BRIEN PRESS
DUBLIN

First published 2006 by The O'Brien Press Ltd,
12 Terenure Road East, Rathgar, Dublin 6, Ireland.
Tel: +353 1 4923333; Fax: +353 1 4922777
E-mail: books@obrien.ie
Website: www.obrien.ie
Reprinted 2006.

ISBN-10: 0-86278-999-0

ISBN-13: 978-0-86278-999-2

Copyright for text © Ralph Riegel 2006

Copyright for typesetting, layout, editing and design
© The O'Brien Press Ltd

The publishers and author thank Provision for all the photographs except that on
page vi (top) which is provided by Gerry Mooney of Independent Newspapers.

All rights reserved. No part of this book may be reproduced or utilised
in any way or by any means, electronic or mechanical, including photocopying,
recording or by any information storage and retrieval system
without permission in writing from the publisher.

British Library Cataloguing-in-Publication Data
Riegel, Ralph
Afraid of the dark : the tragic story of Robert Holohan
1. Holohan, Robert - Death and burial
2. Manslaughter - Ireland
I. Title
364.1'523'092

2 3 4 5 6 7 8 9 10

06 07 08 09 10 11 12

Printing: Nørhaven Paperback A/S

Acknowledgements

This book would not have been possible without the help, generosity and kindness of a great number of people. My biggest thanks go to my long-suffering wife, Mary, my mother, Nora, and my three children, Rachel, Rebecca and Ralph, for allowing me the time, space and peace to complete this work. In more ways that I can detail here, I am truly a lucky man.

My thanks also to Barry Roche of *The Irish Times*, Olivia Kelleher, freelance, Paul Byrne of TV3, Liam Heylin of the *Irish Examiner*, Ann Mooney of the *Irish Daily Mail*, and Mike and Darragh McSweeney and Ted McCarthy of Provision. I am deeply grateful for how generously you all gave of your time and advice in helping me with this project. I am fortunate to have you all as colleagues – but I am honoured to be able to call you friends.

I also have to mention radio reporters Cathy Madden, Fiona Donnelly and Justin McCarthy who covered the search operation in January 2005 and whose detailed reports made life so much easier for those of us in the print media. Thanks also RTÉ's Jennie O'Sullivan for her unstinting help during the search operation itself and to TV3 cameramen, past and present, Ken Fogarty and Rory Fuller, and freelance Niall O'Connor. Thanks also to Patricia Messenger and Cathy Crowley of County Sound/103 FM as well as everyone with the Gerry Ryan Show, Pat Kenny Show and 5-7 Live for their support over the years. Thanks also to Ray Ryan, Dick Cross and Dick Hogan – three great 'mentors'.

My thanks also to Gerry Mooney of Independent Newspapers for kind permission to reproduce award-winning photos of the search for Robert. Thanks too to 96FM and the *Sunday Tribune* for the detailed references to their work included here.

And thanks to all the *Irish Independent* reporters who worked alongside me on this story in various ways over the past nineteen months. These include Tom Brady, Eugene Hogan, Gemma O'Doherty, Helen Bruce, Miriam Lord, Kathy Donaghy, Mark Hilliard, Ann-Marie Walsh and Cormac Looney.

I am also indebted to many others within Independent Newspapers, including Paul Dunne, Dave Halloran, Vinnie Doyle, Gerry O'Regan, Shane Doran, Claire Grady, Don Lavery, Anne-Maria McEneaney, Martha Kearns, Liam Collins, Ciaran Byrne, Willie Kealy, Jody Corcoran, Stephen Rae, Ian Mallon, Barbara Power, Martin Brennan and Mick McCaffrey.

Thanks to Supt Liam Hayes and the many Gardaí who showed so much kindness and forbearance in dealing with various queries over the months. Thanks also to Captain Dan Harvey, Southern Brigade. Thanks to solicitors Frank Buttimer, Ernest Cantillon and Ken Murray for their patience and generosity with their time, often at extremely unsocial hours.

I also have to mention the staff at Cork Library, particularly its reference section, for their incomparable assistance.

I am also deeply grateful for the support and patience of all at The O'Brien Press, including Íde ní Laoghaire, Síne Quinn, Mary Webb and Michael O'Brien. I am slowly learning the lesson that there is indeed a chasm between news reporting and writing a book such as this.

Finally, to Mark and Majella Holohan. I cannot put it any better than Fr Billy O'Donovan in acknowledging that the courage and dignity you both displayed throughout this terrible ordeal was an inspiration to everyone. It is my sincere and heartfelt prayer that time may ease your heavy burden.

Ralph Riegel

Contents

DEDICATION
To the little boy who didn't make it home before dark.

Prologue

The frost still clung to the leaves in the darkest parts of the glen despite the fact it was almost mid-afternoon. The two search volunteers, Martin Sloan and Tom Deely, carefully made their way along the well-worn path examining every bush and briar patch. The cold of that January day in East Cork was apparent in that the fog from their every breath seemed to shroud the small group.

It was clear that the path they were examining was in fairly regular use despite the fact that, in mid-winter, only a hardy few were likely to be venturing onto wind-swept Inch strand. The dog litter that lined the path hinted that most of the people who came here did so to exercise their pets. The isolated Inch beach almost ranked as a closely guarded secret to people in East Cork. Some in the nearby town of Midleton didn't even know the beach existed – preferring to head to more accessible, but crowded strands such as Garryvoe or even Youghal. Inch, though, was popular with surfers who appreciated the strand for its waves.

The day was also surprisingly quiet with the bitterly cold silence broken only by the occasional rustle caused by the searchers examining the frozen undergrowth and the distant sound of a car passing

Leabharlanna Poibli Chathair Baile Átha Cliath
Dublin City Public Libraries

through the crossroads on its way to either Whitegate or Guileen. As a few of the volunteers later recalled: the wild and isolated spot seemed even lonelier that day.

Robert Holohan had now been missing without trace for nine days. The search for the eleven-year-old had escalated from a localised East Cork search operation on 4 January to a national campaign with volunteers from Donegal to Dundalk and from Kerry to Fermanagh offering their services. Ireland was now gripped with the mystery of what had happened to the boy. His fate was dominating newspapers and radio and television stations. The heart-rending appeal by his parents, Mark and Majella, for information on his whereabouts just forty-eight hours before had sparked another flood of volunteers into Midleton to help with the search operation.

Those volunteers, like everyone else nationwide, were mystified as to whether Robert had been abducted or was the victim of a tragic accident. As the days had passed, fears for his safety, and the likelihood of a sinister explanation for his disappearance mounted apace.

Over the previous nine days, every bog, stream, slurry pit, forest and glen in a ten-mile radius around Robert's house at Ballyedmond, northwest of Midleton, had been searched. Some were now being searched for the third time as Gardaí desperately sought to ensure they hadn't missed a single clue as to the boy's whereabouts.

Back at Inch, Martin Sloan and Tom Deely continued their careful search of the woodland. Earlier that morning, a handful of volunteers were told they were going to the Inch and Whitegate areas to continue the search. One Garda said they specifically wanted that area examined. This caused a few raised eyebrows as the volunteers had never heard this type of direction before. Martin and Tom thought no more about it and went where they were asked.

Tom was armed with a stick to cope with the worst of the briars and nettles while Martin had brought along a hurley. Having searched a coastal area of Whitegate over the course of the morning, they relocated to Inch strand for the afternoon. The weather was cold and damp, but both local men knew they only had a couple of hours before it got dark.

The duo were with a small group of volunteers directed by a Garda accompanied by Army personnel. They began examining briars and clumps of undergrowth along the 150 metre pathway leading from the crossroads down to Inch strand. It was an arduous task as, just off the pathway, a steep incline led down to a gully. One misplaced step could result in injury or the painful drop into a deep patch of briars.

Just before 2.00pm, Tom Deely began slashing back at some heavy briars when he stopped in shock. He used his stick to part the bushes and, to his horror, he realised he was staring at a human foot. As he parted the tangle of briars and brambles, he realised that, below the foot, was a leg in black track-suit bottoms. A further glance indicated that, hidden in the thicket, lay a small body.

The two men didn't wait to see any more. They raced back up the pathway to alert the Garda to what they had found. They brought him back and indicated the spot and the briar patch containing the body. Everyone had enough common sense to stay back so as not to interfere with the scene. Within minutes, the Garda radio frequency was buzzing with the news. In the space of one hour, the quiet, isolated crossroads would become the focus of a huge Garda criminal investigation conducted under the spotlight of the national media.

The tragic search for Robert Holohan was finally over.

CHAPTER 1: THE DISAPPEARANCE

TUESDAY, 4 JANUARY 2005
THE DISAPPEARANCE, 2.00PM

Robert Holohan sped out the driveway of his home. His new silver BMX bike kicked up little stones as the wheels spun in response to his urgent desire for speed. Despite the cold of the winter afternoon, his face was flushed with excitement and energy.

It had already been a good day. In fact, it had been a great two weeks. Christmas had brought the marvellous bike that he was now putting through its paces with growing relish. Everyone had liked it – and his friends gave it the ultimate compliment: it was 'cool'. He had also got enough cash in Christmas presents to buy the new Nokia camera phone that he had been admiring in Xtra-vision for weeks. He had agreed to share the phone with his mother, but Robert knew the phone was really his.

The best surprise of all – almost as good as Christmas morning – had been the medal he'd received only two days before from Midleton Gaelic Athletic Association (GAA) club. He'd trained and played with the Midleton underage team over the previous summer and autumn and, like the other lads, he'd been rewarded with a medal.

It was his pride and joy – and, with a jolt, Robert realised that his cherished medal was back in his Ballyedmond house. He'd almost refused to take it off – and he liked the medal so much that he had decided he was now going to concentrate on horses and hurling, his two great loves. Never mind, he thought, he'd pick up his medal later when he came back home for tea. Now it was time for some fun and to find his friends.

The morning had already been good. He'd built a special ramp on the driveway of his Ballyedmond home and practised jumping over it with his new bike. This BMX was much better than a racer, he thought, with tyres that were perfect for the local roads and lanes where he loved to play.

3.30PM

Majella Holohan was just about to start preparing the family tea when she thought that she'd call Robert to see what he wanted to eat. She tried him on his new mobile, but couldn't get any answer. The phone just rang out.

She thought no more about it – and decided to try him again in a few minutes. Her other children, Emma (eight) and Harry (four), were happily playing around the house. Perhaps Robert didn't hear the phone. But it was unusual for him to be so long away from the house without letting her know where he was. 'We always kept in contact – just to see what he was up to,' Majella said.

A few minutes later, after again failing to get any answer from Robert, she decided to leave a message on the mobile. 'Rob, it's Mam, give me a buzz'. By 5.00pm Majella had still failed to make contact with her son despite ringing his phone at least six times. With darkness falling she was becoming increasingly worried. 'Rob didn't like the dark. In fact, he hated the dark. He always made sure he was home before it got dark. That's why I was getting worried,' she said.

5.30PM

By 5.30pm her husband, Mark, had returned home from work and was greeted by a worried Majella. The family immediately began to try and locate their missing son. While they were concerned, they didn't think for a moment that anything untoward had happened. After all, this was Ballyedmond: it was quiet, rural and all the neighbours looked out for each other.

Majella decided to send her daughter, Emma, around to some of the neighbours' houses to try and find out where Robert was. One of the first houses that Emma called to was their immediate neighbours, the O'Donoghues, where Robert was a frequent visitor. But the family's eldest son, Wayne (twenty), said he hadn't seen Robert since before lunch. Wayne was one of Robert's heroes – Robert's grandfather, William Murray, said that the eleven-year-old thought that the older boy was some kind of God. Wayne's house was one of Robert's favourite places – and if he wasn't there, where could he have gone to on his bike?

While Emma was calling to the immediate neighbours, Majella had started working the phone in a bid to discover Robert's whereabouts. The more people she rang, the more worried she became. No one had seen Robert. At least not since before lunch that day. Where could he be? Mark and Majella decided to get into the family jeep and start a trawl of Robert's favourite spots around the East Cork town. They went to McDonald's in Midleton, then the GAA club and even a local leisure centre, Fat Als, where Robert often went with his friends. But there was no trace of their son. No one had seen him around town that afternoon. It was as if he had disappeared into thin air.

Majella then began a desperate ring-around of Robert's school friends – even those living some distance from Ballyedmond. Could the eleven-year-old possibly have decided to travel into town on his bike and simply lost track of the time?

7.00PM

By now both Mark and Majella were beginning to panic and decided they had to alert the Gardaí. Garda Liam Ryan and Sergeant Jim O'Leary responded to the call to Midleton station and decided to travel to Ballyedmond to assess the situation for themselves. 'There was already a number of people out searching,' Garda Ryan recalled. These included Mark and Majella Holohan as well as a number of the immediate neighbours in Ballyedmond.

The Gardaí consulted with the Holohan family and began to coordinate the search effort. They decided that a methodical approach had to be adopted and began door-to-door inquiries in Ballyedmond to try and discover Robert's last movements. Their immediate superiors, Supt Liam Hayes and Inspector Martin Dorney, were briefed on developments.

As the Garda inquiries began to progress, it emerged that while a number of people in the area had seen Robert before lunchtime, no one had seen him after 3.00pm.

9.00PM

Shortly after 9.00pm, the Gardaí got their first break when it emerged that a local man and his son, Tom Keohane Snr and Thomas Keohane Jnr, had spotted a silver bike lying in the ditch earlier that evening in Ballyedmond as they were returning home.

'My son said it was a new bike. We said we'd bring it home and have a look at it and see who it belonged to. Later, I saw a sticker on the bike saying "An Rothar", a local bike shop,' Tom Keohane said. Thinking that the bike had been misplaced or forgotten, the father and son decided to bring it back to their home and try to discover who owned it.

'It was placed against the ditch,' Thomas Keohane Jnr said. 'It was parked neatly. It was a one-size-for-all bike, but the saddle was low.'

After hearing about the discovery of the bike, the Gardaí decided to try and confirm that it did, in fact, belong to Robert. They consulted with the Holohans and Majella asked Robert's friend, Wayne, to go and identify the bike. A short time later he returned to say that the bike was definitely the silver BMX that the eleven-year-old had received for Christmas. A straightforward missing person's case had just got far more serious.

Gardaí fears mounted when they realised just how much the bike meant to Robert. On one occasion, the boy had gone to McDonald's and bluntly refused to leave his beloved BMX outside on the street even though he could see it through the glass window. If this was how much the silver bike meant to Robert, would he have willingly abandoned it in a ditch beside a road? Privately, Gardaí began to fear the worst.

11.00PM

By now the word had spread around Ballyedmond and parts of Midleton that a local boy was missing. Nothing travels as fast in rural Ireland as the word that a local is in trouble. And the local community quickly pulled together. Neighbours as well as members of the GAA and hunting clubs began arriving to see what they could do. Most arrived with weather-proof gear and flashlights. Friends of the Holohans moved into their home to try and support the family by answering phones and trying desperately to think of places where Robert might have gone.

Others came because they knew Robert. Pat Healy (who runs a livery yard at Ballyspillane) called to the Holohan home to see what he could do. 'There were about twenty people outside the house and they were beginning to search,' he explained. Pat recalled seeing people in reflective jackets armed with torches beginning to search the fields and ditches.

Outside, the beams of flashlights split the darkness around the rural area. Locals initially targeted the woods, laneways, ditches and glens in the belief that Robert might have suffered an accident. All of Robert's favourite spots, his so-called 'cabbys', were searched, but to no avail. The Keohanes brought the Gardaí to the exact spot where the bike had been found and search teams began spreading out across the fields to try and discover some trace of Robert.

Another search volunteer, John Ansbro, recalled how people were desperately trying to figure out where the boy could have gone. Mr Ansbro also recalled seeing Wayne O'Donoghue out searching that night. 'Wayne said he must have fallen off his bike,' he added. 'I saw him [Wayne] on the following night in the Garda station. He told me he had been up all night searching.'

Wayne wasn't the only neighbour involved in the search. The entire O'Donoghue family, led by Wayne's father, Ray, had arrived to try and help. Other neighbours began making flasks of tea and coffee for the search volunteers. As the hours passed and there was still no trace of Robert, Midleton Gardaí increasingly began to fear that hopes of an early and happy resolution to the crisis might be in vain.

MIDNIGHT

The search operation continued beyond midnight and through to the early hours of Wednesday morning, 5 January. As weary volunteers began to head home for some rest, there was still no trace of Robert nor any idea of what had happened to him. By lunchtime that day, word of the disappearance had spread through Midleton and East Cork.

News of the search operation was broadcast, for the first time, on Cork local radio stations and, slowly but surely, the search for Robert became a national campaign.

By late afternoon, news of the young boy's disappearance was carried on RTÉ, TV3, local and Dublin radio stations and the *Irish Independent*, *The Irish Times* and the *Irish Examiner* were working on the story for their editions of the next day. By that Wednesday afternoon, the first television crews began to converge on Ballyedmond and the decision was made to use the nearby East Cork Golf Club as the coordination centre for the search effort. The hunt for Robert was about to become a national campaign and ignite the solidarity of an entire community.

CHAPTER 2: THE SEARCH

WEDNESDAY, 5 JANUARY 2005
THE SEARCH, DAY TWO

The Christmas lights were still twinkling along Cork's South Mall and, despite the darkness of the early January evening, there was a definite air of excitement in the city centre. Cork was beginning its reign as EU Capital of Culture for 2005, and the weekend promised a feast of entertainment for singles and families alike. There was a huge fireworks spectacular, a special theatre pageant on the river Lee and a host of open-air attractions, from musicians to street-theatre performances. It was a good time to be in Cork.

At 3.00pm that day I was walking along the South Mall with my wife, Mary, and three children, anticipating the weekend events to come. In fact, the only worry I had was about getting enough tickets for the fireworks display that evening to cater for my own children and their cousins. I was off-duty and relieved that any breaking news concerns of the *Irish Independent* and *Evening Herald* weren't mine. At least, so I thought.

As southern correspondent for the *Irish Independent* I'd been on duty for much of the Christmas and New Year period and was enjoying a few lazy days off. Olivia Kelleher, a Cork freelance reporter, was on duty for me and I was in the city with my family checking out the January sales.

Just then my mobile phone rang and, despite a disapproving look from my wife, I broke my own rule about answering the phone on a day off. It was Don Lavery, the news editor of the *Irish Independent*, and my day-off was about to be revoked. 'Do you know about the young lad who is missing in Midleton?' Don asked. I replied that I had heard about the Garda search but, as the boy was only missing for twenty-four hours, I had opted to leave the story with Olivia and await developments, if necessary coming back on duty at a moment's notice. 'I'm sorry to do this, but I think it would be better if you came back on duty, just in case,' Don apologised.

Over the previous nine years working as a regional beat reporter based in Cork, I'd covered numerous missing children stories. Some were appalling tragedies where youngsters had fallen into slurry pits or rivers. In many of these cases it was almost immediately apparent that the Garda operation was more a recovery than a rescue mission.

On other occasions, the missing youngster would turn up hours or sometimes even days later at a friend's house or even in a bed-and-breakfast. I recall one particular case of a three-year-old boy going missing in West Cork and, more than thirty-six hours after he disappeared, then turning up safe and well in a hay barn. The youngster had simply wandered off to play with some animals and, when tired, had found a haybarn and gone to sleep for the night. He was tired, but none the worse for wear after his ordeal. When his relieved parents asked him where he had been, without a hint of a smile, he simply replied: 'Brazil.'

Other cases were marked by more sinister overtones: the fear that the disappearance could be in some way linked to paedophilia. But in twenty-one years working in journalism in Cork, Dublin and Waterford I'd never encountered a case of a deliberate child abduction. Tragically, there had been too many cases to count in which offenders were before the Circuit Criminal Court for sexually motivated assaults on youngsters, but none involved abductions or disappearances. That was the primary concern in my mind as I agreed to head to East Cork to begin work on the story.

As I came back on duty, I wondered whether this story might have a happy ending. As I left my own youngsters in the packed city centre, I was already wondering about what precisely was involved in the Midleton disappearance. Either way, I had to get out of Cork city and head to East Cork as soon as possible if I was to have a detailed story by our early edition deadlines.

Even though I'm from Fermoy, which is just twenty miles from Midleton, I'd never been to Ballyedmond. Ironically enough, the townland is located just off the Midleton to Fermoy road, less than two miles from the centre of the prosperous East Cork town. It was easy enough to find; my Garda contact had simply said take the turn by the East Cork oil depot, climb the steep hill and Ballyedmond is on the left-hand side. By the time I arrived it was already dark and it was clear that a major search operation had been underway for some time.

Gardaí manned a portion of the Ballyedmond road where, I discovered, the missing boy lived. Having made a few calls to colleagues and Garda contacts, I discovered that the search was already being coordinated from Midleton Garda station and the East Cork golf club, whose premises are less than one mile from the Holohan home. Amongst the senior Gardaí already liaising with the search volunteers were Supt Liam Hayes and Inspector Martin Dorney, two men I already knew through District Court cases over the years. If anyone would find the boy, I reckoned, these officers would.

At that stage, there was widespread confusion about what exactly might be involved in the disappearance. The majority of speculation seemed to revolve around a tragic accident, possibly involving the nearby river that runs along the bottom of fields to the rear of the Holohan home. Because of the season and the quantity of heavy rainfall over previous weeks, the sedate river now closely resembled a torrent rather than a quiet stream. The odd flash of light from lamps indicated

that volunteers were already searching along the riverbank and probing the freezing waters. While Ballyedmond is a typical farming area,
there are also plenty of glens, forests and areas of scrubland where
someone injured in an accident might find it difficult to raise the alarm.

The unspoken fear – as it always is in these cases – was that of an
abduction. There appeared to be no witnesses suggesting that Robert
had been snatched and no one had seen anything remotely suspicious
in Ballyedmond either on 4 January or any previous days. I already
knew that Robert's bike had been found a couple of hundred metres
from his home, placed in a ditch. The question remained whether the
bike was placed there by a boy who was going rambling or dumped by
someone else with more sinister motives.

It was abundantly clear that the Gardaí and the Midleton community
were taking nothing for granted. The scene at the East Cork golf club,
even at that late stage in the afternoon, was one of frenetic activity.
Dozens of people milled around, almost all clad in warm, weather-
proof clothing. Everyone had either hiking boots or Wellingtons on.
Despite the darkness, it was clear that some people were determined to
search on until the boy was found. My Garda contacts quickly made it
clear that they were keeping all their options open. This could be a
tragic accident with a body waiting to be found in a river or stream. Or
it could equally involve something far more sinister. The simply reality
was, just twenty-four hours after Robert disappeared, Gardaí just
didn't know which way their investigation would go.

THURSDAY, 6 JANUARY 2005
THE SEARCH, DAY THREE

As the third day of the search dawned, the media interest in the disappearance intensified and with it came a wave of volunteers from all
over Ireland. To this day, experienced Gardaí like Liam Hayes and
Martin Dorney still can't pinpoint exactly when the search operation

'went national'. Gardaí and even the Holohan family were taken aback at how quickly a trickle of search volunteers turned into a flood.

For many, it was the emotion generated by Majella Holohan's first heartbreaking appeal for information on her son which was broadcast that afternoon via the two main television correspondents in Cork: Paschal Sheehy for RTÉ and Paul Byrne for TV3. For others, it was the sight of then-Hurler of the Year and Cork All-Ireland star, Seán Óg Ó hAilpín, lending his weight to the search mission that sparked the decision to help. Robert had lots of heroes, largely in the equestrian and hurling worlds. But no one was as special to the boy as Seán Óg. A poster of the Na Piarsaigh star had pride of place on his bedroom wall. Seán Óg was Robert's favourite player on the Cork hurling team despite the fact that many star players on that side lived closer to Midleton than Ó hAilpín.

The minute Seán Óg heard about the disappearance and the fact that the missing boy held him in awe, he contacted Midleton GAA club to offer whatever help he could. That night, a special appeal for information on Robert's whereabouts was broadcast by the Cork hurling star.

He wasn't the only sports star trying to help out: former Cork and Midleton hurling star, Kevin Hennessy, an official with the Revenue Commissioners, took part in the search effort, while Cork's 1999 All-Ireland winning hurling captain, Mark Landers, also joined the search. Mark knew the Holohan family through his job with the Permanent TSB bank, and he wanted to do something to help. 'When people began to realise how serious the situation was, everyone wanted to play their part with the search. It's the only thing people are talking about in Midleton today and the whole place is out searching,' he said.

The same evening, Majella Holohan tried to explain to a stunned Irish public what had happened in East Cork. Majella wept as she pleaded for the safe return of her son. 'Whoever has him please let him go and send him home to me tonight. We want him home tonight with us,' she sobbed. 'It is devastating for our family. I can't put into words how hard it is. Robert is our eldest child and we love him so very, very much. All we want is for him to be back home safe with us. I want him back home,' she added.

The Cork mother of three said their fears had been mounting as the hours passed without word of Robert's whereabouts. 'Well, as the days are going on we are getting worried and we just don't know. Maybe somebody took him. But I am afraid that he has fallen and hit his head. You know, he just seems to have disappeared. We are not sure really at this stage. We are totally baffled,' she explained to the media. 'We can't sleep and we are not eating. We just can't believe that this has happened. Everybody in Midleton knows Robert. He is a very happy boy and loves talking to people. He loves animals and horses. He loves his bike. He is opinionated, just like every eleven-year-old, but he is a lovely, kind boy.' The family admitted their fears were worsened by the knowledge that such a disappearance was totally out of character for Robert – and the treatment of his beloved BMX was a particular cause for concern.

'He is actually scared of the dark so even if he was down at a friend's house, just next door, we would have to go down and walk back up with him,' Majella explained. And just minutes before he left home on Tuesday, Robert had been polishing his beloved BMX. 'He loved that bike. He was cleaning it that morning. He was always working on it. It was a silver BMX bike that he got for Christmas. It was out in the rain one night and he ran out and put it in the porch,' she said. Majella said she couldn't believe it when Robert failed to return home on 4 January, and then failed to answer his mobile. 'I rang him to ask him what he wanted for his dinner and to tell him to come in and it just rang out. I rang him again at 4.30pm and then at 4.45pm and it [Robert's mobile] went to the answering machine, but I kept ringing. When Mark came home at 5.30pm. we were worried because we know he hates the dark.' Mark, Robert's dad, said that the family now feared the worst – that their son was taken against his will. 'I fear he may have been abducted – what else can I think? He has been gone so long,' he said.

Yet, as the search operation escalated into a national campaign, the Gardaí remained baffled as to what exactly had happened to Robert. There was absolutely no sign of a struggle or a disturbance in the area where the bike had been found. Despite a huge search over the previous forty-eight hours of the entire Ballyedmond area, including the draining of some ponds and slurry pits, there hadn't been a single trace of the youngster found.

For Supt Hayes, it was now a race against time and the weather. 'He has been missing now for over forty-eight hours and we have had two very cold nights since then. We would now have serious concerns for Robert's welfare,' he told the media at East Cork golf club.

There was also the growing concern amongst Gardaí that someone knew more about Robert's disappearance than they were saying. Gardaí didn't believe that a healthy, strong eleven-year-old boy could literally vanish into thin air. Someone had to have seen something – even if, perhaps, they didn't realise its full significance. If that person knew something and was deliberately withholding the information, then the Garda operation would take an alarmingly different course.

The third full day of the search for Robert had featured personnel including members of the Gardaí, Midleton GAA club, the Defence Forces, Irish Coastguard and the Civil Defence. Specialist dog handlers had offered their services as had members of local hunts who were familiar with the heavily forested terrain around Ballyedmond. Even a helicopter equipped with special heat-sensitive equipment had swept the general area.

The search operation was now going to be dramatically expanded – having been focused over the previous forty-eight hours on a five-mile area around Robert's home. Commandant Dan Harvey of the Southern Brigade stressed that Defence Forces personnel specially equipped to search heavy scrubland and wooded areas were now assisting Gardaí.

'We are doing everything we possibly can to assist the search and, like the Gardaí, we are hoping and praying that the little boy will be found safe and well,' he said.

Given the fears that Robert might have suffered a water-related accident, the Naval Service also provided personnel. A special Naval Service diving team – led by Lieutenant Tony O'Regan – had joined the search and, together with members of the Garda sub-aqua unit, continued to search drains, rivers and wells in the area. Within days they too were joined by volunteers from sub-aqua clubs all over Cork and Munster.

FRIDAY, 7 JANUARY 2005
THE SEARCH, DAY FOUR

The campaign to find Robert was now the dominant news item in Ireland. It was on every hourly news bulletin; it was on the front page of virtually every Irish newspaper and it had even made some British papers. Crucially, hundreds of volunteers were now arriving in Midleton to assist the Garda search operation, some having travelled from as far as Sligo, Donegal, Belfast and Dublin.

There was now a permanent media presence in both Midleton and Ballyedmond at the East Cork golf club. The local papers, the *Irish Examiner* and the *Evening Echo*, were giving the story blanket coverage and had numerous reporters assigned to various aspects of the search. Reporters from Cork's local radio stations, 96FM, Red FM and County Sound were also filing hourly updates on the search for Robert.

But now, for the first time, people were beginning to notice the dramatic impact the search was having on the community. At first, the signs were small. I saw a man in a jeep pull up outside the East Cork golf club, open the rear of his 4x4 and take out an armful of Christmas selection boxes and carry them into the clubhouse. I strolled over to one of the Gardaí on duty and discreetly asked where the guy was going. It transpired that the man owned a petrol station in Midleton and had a large number of unsold selection boxes left over from Christmas. He had donated the lot to the canteen set up for the search volunteers.

And then the trickle of donations became a flood as East Cork communities almost appeared to make a conscious effort to try and ensure that something decent came out of something so terrible. I saw one old lady carefully carrying a large tin-foil-wrapped tray up through the car-park towards the clubhouse. A radio reporter spoke to her as she left later and I heard that the woman wasn't physically able to help with the search mission or the car-park operation, but she could cook and she had a spare ham left from Christmas. She'd brought the cooked and lovingly prepared ham to the clubhouse so it could be used for sandwiches. And she went home knowing she had played her part.

Another man who had a bad hip and couldn't manage the search either, insisted that he was well enough to help the Civil Defence with car-parking duties. A number of drinks companies instructed their reps to drop off cartons of soft drinks at Ballyedmond for the search volunteers. It was a mood of selflessness and community that, in the trying days to come, Midleton would try to hold onto as a hope for better times.

Away from the clubhouse, the exhausting task of searching the countryside continued. If the abduction fear was unspoken over the first twenty-four hours of the search mission it was now to the forefront of every mind. East Cork Gardaí were now checking on known sex offenders. Within days this would become one of the dominant revelations of the entire search effort.

Gardaí also stressed, for the first time, that while they were still keeping an open mind about Robert's disappearance, they were now treating the matter as a criminal investigation. It also emerged that East Cork officers were now being assisted by members of the elite National Bureau of Criminal Investigations (NBCI) amid mounting fears of an abduction.

Mark Holohan, unable to bear the waiting, was working around-the-clock to assist the search operation. For Mark and Majella, the previous three days had proved an exhausting ordeal. A Nokia mobile phone had been found in a ditch near the river, but it transpired that the phone was not Robert's and had been lost by a person out walking some weeks before. Gardaí had received four vague sightings which they initially thought might have been of Robert. Sadly, all were subsequently discounted.

Midleton Gardaí had taken copies of all CCTV security-camera footage from around the town and examined it for any clue as to Robert's movements. Unfortunately, there was no trace of the boy, but Gardaí did discover clues as to the movements of another individual in Ballyedmond that day – a fact that would not emerge as crucial for several days.

The search operation was now focused on a sprawling twenty-four square miles of countryside, some of it virtual wilderness, covered in briars and gorse, and deep, fast-flowing streams and gullies. Every derelict building in that search zone was combed, and several slurry pits were now being emptied for the second time, but there was still no trace of Robert.

SATURDAY, 8 JANUARY 2005
THE SEARCH, DAY FIVE

East Cork, let alone Midleton, had never seen anything like it. Over three thousand volunteers and emergency service personnel were now out on the search mission. The crowds arriving in the town were so great that special traffic and parking arrangements had to be put in place around the East Cork golf club. Off-duty Gardaí from around Ireland drove to East Cork to try and help their Midleton colleagues while the Defence Forces deployed their reserves through the 23rd and

13th Infantry Battalions. By mid-afternoon, Army personnel drawn from Cork, Kilkenny, Tipperary and Limerick were actively involved in the search.

But that wasn't all: East Cork golf club now resembled a military installation with the members' bar converted into a canteen where freezing, wet and exhausted volunteers could have a hot drink and some food. Senior Garda officers maintained a special briefing room where detailed Ordnance Survey maps of the countryside were erected to allow search areas to be checked and monitored.

The search had already been boosted by an appeal from National Association of Regional Game Councils (NARGC) boss, Michael O'Keeffe, for local members to directly help the Gardaí. Because of the nature of their sport, few people knew woodland or the wilderness as well as NARGC members. Michael O'Keeffe later appealed to council members throughout Munster to do whatever they could to support the search for Robert. 'We want to broaden the search to our members throughout Munster. All our members, particularly in the Munster region, are now asked to help support the search which is already being supported by our members in Cork.'

Local TD David Stanton (FG), an East Cork native, personally took part in the search effort and said that the Gardaí and civil powers were doing everything possible to help trace Robert. 'We are all very concerned and very, very worried for Robert. But we just have to keep at it and pray that we will find something,' he said.

For Mark and Majella, the ordeal simply seemed to get worse and they feared news almost as much as they hated not knowing what had happened to their son. 'It's a nightmare – what else can I say,' Mark Holohan said. 'I never thought I would see myself involved in something like this. It never happens on your own door. It's something you see on telly but never in your own home, your own community.'

And as the huge search operation failed to yield results, even the most unusual avenues were being considered. Two psychics had contacted the search leaders and offered their services and East Cork Gardaí insisted that 'every piece of information is welcomed and will be checked.' And then there were the volunteers who kept flooding into East Cork to offer help. Their numbers had rocketed on Friday afternoon as people decided to devote their weekend to searching for Robert.

John Moore from Edenderry in County Offaly was watching the search on television and just felt he had to do something. 'I was sitting at home watching it the first night and I was thinking, this was desperate. But it's one thing just to sit there and think how desperate it is, and it is totally another to get up and do something about it. So I came down to help out,' he explained.

TJ Dunne, a building contractor from Sligo, had planned to go golfing for the weekend with some mates but, on Friday night, decided to change his plans and drive to Cork to see if he could help. 'I have a friend who is a Garda and he had been telling me all about the search for Robert. I watched it on the news and I suppose I realised that it could so easily have been one of my kids. I decided to come down and see if I could help. It's no big deal,' he said.

SUNDAY, 9 JANUARY 2005
THE SEARCH, DAY SIX

It was fitting that as the search entered its sixth day on Sunday, the emphasis was as much on prayer as it was on scouring the countryside. Fr Billy O'Donovan, Midleton's curate, decided to organise a special ecumenical 'ceremony of hope' in the Church of the Holy Rosary to show solidarity with the Holohan family and to allow a worried community an outlet for their concerns.

The service attracted hundreds of Midleton locals and search volunteers with Fr O'Donovan inviting Mark and Majella onto the altar to light a special candle of hope. This candle, he vowed, would remain lit until Robert was found. Few knew it that evening but Fr O'Donovan's promise would come true, but in a tragically different sense.

'The disappearance has shocked our entire community. But we are praying both for the Holohan family and for Robert's safe return,' Fr O'Donovan declared. Midleton's canon, Fr Bertie Troy, pleaded with people not to give up hope and to continue their sterling support for the search campaign. 'We would urge people to continue to support the Gardaí – and to pray for Robert's family and for his safe return home,' Fr Troy said. 'Robert's parents are waiting and praying for that phone call that their son is safe.' Fr Padraig Keogh, Midleton parish priest, also stressed that 'There is always hope.'

But the faith of the Gardaí, Army personnel and search volunteers was being sorely tested. I arrived in the car-park of the East Cork golf club amid driving rain and gusting winds. I got soaked running just the 100 metres or so from my car into the clubhouse to meet Gardaí for an update. I couldn't imagine what it must have been like for people out searching in gullies amid gorse and briar patches. Those that I could see trudging stoically back to the clubhouse for a cup of tea and a sandwich were armed with either walking poles or hurleys, anything to try and search through the briars and nettles.

I met Sean O'Riordan, the crime correspondent for the *Irish Examiner*, inside the golf club. Like myself, Sean was shocked by the conditions being braved by Gardaí and search volunteers alike. As we sat inside the clubhouse chatting to Gardaí about the latest details of the operation, volunteers trudged in and out, soaked and frozen but determined to keep on searching.

It was also abundantly clear that the Gardaí and Army were worried about the weather conditions – and particularly the implications for safety once the light began to fade. Commandant Dan Harvey, a longtime friend of mine, admitted to me afterwards that the search conditions were as bad as any he had ever known. And yet hundreds stayed out in the appalling weather, all unpaid and most on weekends away from work, just to try and help the Holohans. 'I've never seen anything like it in my life,' said Captain Harvey, himself a father-of-four.

Gene O'Sullivan, a former member of the Defence Forces' elite Rangers unit, explained that many of those ignoring the weather conditions to take part in the search effort were parents. Gene (who lives in nearby Castlemartyr) said he had an eleven-year-old and couldn't imagine being in the position the Holohans now faced. 'My daughter once went missing for twenty minutes when I was in town and everything went through my head. I know exactly what those poor people are going through. That is why I am here to do everything that I can to help,' he said.

Over the weekend, Gardaí liaised with all landowners within the search radius who were asked to drain slurry tanks to aid their detailed examination. Likewise, Naval personnel and sub-aqua groups were now extending their search of the swollen Owenacurra river, which effectively runs north of Ballyedmond, parallel to the Midleton-Fermoy road, to stretches as far away as Lisgoold. The conditions were so demanding that volunteers in the river, searching deep pools and bank overhangs, had to wear safety ropes for fear of being swept away on the current and the flood waters.

CHAPTER 3: THE SEARCH CONTINUES

MONDAY, 10 JANUARY 2005
THE SEARCH, DAY SEVEN

An improvement in the weather was greeted with relief by the searchers who once again flocked to the East Cork golf club. It had been a tough weekend for everyone, especially the Holohan family as they had awaited the results of desperate Garda efforts to trace down every lead and every potential piece of evidence. Once again, search volunteers strode through fields, bushes and forestry as the clatter of rotors overhead indicated that the Garda Aerial Support Unit was once again in the area.

At lunchtime, Midleton Gardaí released a photo of Robert taken only eighteen hours before his disappearance as he proudly accepted a Midleton GAA under-twelve hurling medal. Critically, the photo showed Robert wearing the black Nike top he was wearing on the day he disappeared. Midleton detectives were hoping the picture would help refresh the memory of someone in the East Cork area that day. Until now, the Gardaí and, via them, the media, were depending on two photos that had been issued on 5 January, the second day of the search. One showed Robert in a swimming pool while on holidays; the second picture was from a family trip to Santa Claus. The GAA photo was up-to-date.

The mounting shock over Robert's disappearance had also prompted Gardaí to support the sending of a team of psychologists to the eleven-year-old's school, Midleton CBS, to offer support and counselling for any of his classmates or their parents. The school, which resumed classes on 10 January after the Christmas break, also offered prayers for Robert's safe return.

Crucially, Supt Liam Hayes stated that one possible witness had now been eliminated from the Garda inquiry. Detectives learned that a woman with brown hair, aged between thirty-five and forty, had been seen walking the previous Tuesday in the Waterock area of Midleton not far from where the eleven-year-old had disappeared. An appeal was issued for this woman – and Gardaí initially hoped that she might have seen Robert or anything suspicious in the area. On Sunday the woman contacted Gardaí and, after an interview, was totally eliminated from the inquiry as not having seen Robert or anything of significance.

Gardaí again renewed their appeals for anyone driving a white Transit or Hiace-type van in the Midleton area that Tuesday to contact them. A number of callers to Gardaí had reported seeing such vehicles, of various types, in the general area and Gardaí now wanted to dismiss them from their inquiries.

Gardaí insisted that the search operation would continue as Garda Commissioner Noel Conroy vowed that extra manpower would be provided for the East Cork Division if required. 'Whatever resources are needed will be provided – we will provide every resource possible to help bring Robert home safe,' he stated.

To date, the hunt for Robert had been led by Supt Liam Hayes and Chief Supt Kieran McGann; they were now to be assisted by two experienced Assistant Commissioners, Adrian Culligan and Tony Hickey. Commissioner Hickey, one of the most experienced investigators in the force, was head of the elite National Bureau of Criminal Investigations (NBCI) and their involvement in the operation raised serious fears about what Gardaí expected to find.

The search radius now being combed by volunteers had been extended to almost twelve miles outside Midleton, with particular attention being paid to streams and river valleys. Some areas had been searched three times – and the intensive nature of the search was borne out by the fact that one search team even uncovered a half kilogram of cannabis resin that had been carefully concealed in a ditch.

A number of lost mobile phones were also found, but none confirmed as being Robert's new Nokia 3200. The fact that a host of discarded items in ditches, streams and glens had also been examined – ranging from old handbags to a Wellington boot – emphasised the scale of the search. Unfortunately, none was in any way connected to Robert. While Gardaí insisted the probe was still a missing person's hunt, increasing emphasis was being placed on fears that Robert was abducted. Anyone with convictions for sexual offences and all those listed on the Sex Offenders Register who were living in the East Cork area were now being visited by Gardaí to determine their movements that Tuesday. It was a disturbing development and was given prominence in both radio and newspaper reports.

Poignantly, the day ended with another heartbreaking appeal from Mark and Majella Holohan for information on what had happened to their son. The couple stressed that they wanted to speak out just to thank the thousands of people, from all over Ireland, who had tried to help in their desperate search for Robert. They said they were now 'clinging to hope' that Robert was still alive and would eventually return to them. But Mark said the couple and their other two children had been going through an absolute nightmare since Robert disappeared. 'We still think it's 50-50. The simple fact that he [Robert] has not been found by now – that is what's giving us the faith that he is still alive.'

The Holohans explained that, had Robert fallen victim to a tragic accident such as a hit-and-run or an even more sinister fate, the huge search operation would surely have discovered his body by now. 'There's been a massive search going on in the area – thousands of people have hunted through it. It really has been thoroughly searched so we're beginning to feel that if it is a hit-and-run or if somebody had murdered him, then Robert would surely have been found by now.'

As time passed and with still no word of Robert's welfare or where-abouts, his parents said they were left with only one fear and belief – that he was abducted. 'We're just hoping that he's inside in a house with somebody at this stage and that he is unharmed and alive,' Mark said. 'We're just praying that Robert will show up alive here. We want our son back. We want him safe and back home.'

Majella said that their pain and anguish had increased each day with no word of their son. 'Well, as the days are going on we are getting more and more worried. We just don't know. Maybe somebody took him. We are not sure really at this stage. We are totally baffled.' She acknowledged that the toll exacted on the family had been enormous – despite the best efforts of friends, neighbours and family to ease their burden. 'We can't sleep and we are not eating. We just can't believe that this has happened. We're totally shocked.'

Majella once again appealed to anyone who might be holding her son to release him and allow him return to the family that loved him so much. The only bright note for the family had been the incredible out-pouring of support, prayers, sympathy and practical help from neigh-bours, friends and even people they didn't know who had been moved by their plight. The Holohan family said that they had been stunned by the generosity and kindness of their neighbours and the thousands of volunteers who travelled to East Cork to help with the search for their son. Mark Holohan was very moved by the incredible decency of people. 'I'd like to thank everyone here who has been looking for Robert. I know now that I may not have been seen down on the search myself because I'm so busy up here doing interviews and things and I just can't do everything.'

'I can't go searching and talking to people at the same time. That's why all the help is so fantastic,' he continued. 'There's a massive number of people out. There's been the Army, the Gardaí, the Civil Defence and a lot of ordinary lads who took time off work to help.' He went on to pay particular tribute to Supt Liam Hayes who had led the search for Robert and the rank-and-file Gardaí, some of whom had even postponed leave and holidays to support the search effort. 'I want to thank them all from the bottom of my heart – and even all the people who have been bringing in food into the golf club for those working on the search.'

TUESDAY, 11 JANUARY 2005
THE SEARCH, DAY EIGHT

I met Paul Byrne from TV3 early that day as I arrived in Midleton. I knew he had been busy on the case over the previous days but he explained that he'd also been working to try and help Gardaí arrange a reconstruction of Robert's last movements. From a television perspective, such an event was of huge interest, and from a Garda viewpoint it could prove crucial in jogging memories and providing a potentially valuable visual aid to people in East Cork of exactly what Robert looked like and the precise area in which he had last been seen.

Crucially, it was now a full week since Robert had disappeared, and despite one of the biggest search operations ever mounted by Gardaí in modern times, not a single trace of the boy had been found. There were no sightings after 2.30pm, there was no forensic evidence of where he might have gone and the trawl of fields, rivers and forests had yielded nothing. Gardaí still had very little to work with: no forensics to analyse, no scene to process and no sightings of Robert – but they were about to get the breakthrough they so badly needed.

Gardaí felt a reconstruction of Robert's last movements could jog a few memories and bring forward some crucial new evidence. Paul

Byrne had organised a young boy to act as Robert who was the same height, and had the same build and hair colour as Robert. The boy was twelve years old and was from Cork city. His family had readily agreed to let him co-operate with the reconstruction if it would help the Holohans get their son back. Once Gardaí gave the official go-ahead, they secured a bike identical to the one Robert was using as well as Midleton GAA tracksuit bottoms, Nike runners and a black jacket similar to those that Robert wearing seven days earlier.

It was hoped to stage the reconstruction at Ballyedmond over lunchtime to best replicate the conditions when Robert disappeared, and the Holohan family had agreed to allow the reconstruction team use their home and driveway. I went to the East Cork golf club to see what other developments were likely but was simply told that the search was ongoing and that nothing of significance had been found. There was an improvement in the weather and for this everyone was grateful.

The search teams were now combing a huge area of East Cork: some of the volunteers were being dispatched to places as far as twelve and fourteen miles from Ballyedmond. For the first time, I heard Whitegate, south of Midleton on the coast, being mentioned as one of the search areas. The search was even being supported by special engineer units from the Southern Brigade at Collins Barracks in Cork, with teams trained in examining wells, caves and fast-flowing rivers, areas not easily accessible to ordinary search personnel.

Gardaí were again trying to eliminate sightings in the Midleton area from their investigation list and were also looking for a jogger who had been spotted on the Ballyedmond road, as well as the owner of a red Transit-type van seen on the Fermoy road out of Midleton.

Shortly before lunch, I drove the short distance from the golf club up to where the Holohans lived and was greeted by a gathering of photographers and reporters. Both TV3 and RTÉ had sent crews and the reconstruction was already certain to dominate the evening television news. Little did we all know that those images filmed on Ballyedmond

Hill that day would be repeatedly broadcast for months to come to illustrate ongoing events in the story. And as we chatted while waiting for the reconstruction to begin, we learned that the Holohans were going to make another appeal for information on Robert's whereabouts. When that appeal finally came, it was clear that the Mark and Majella were now convinced their son had not suffered an accident, and had been abducted. They were now praying he was still alive, and pleading with whoever took Robert to let him go.

'I am thinking he [Robert] has been moved from the Midleton area. I am just thinking at this stage he must have been bundled into a van and taken from the area,' Majella said. It was clear to all that the mother-of-three was now under enormous emotional stress and was steeling herself for the worst.

'Whoever did this is not on his own, by himself. Maybe this was a prank that got out of hand. Maybe because of the media speculation and the helicopter and the searches that they could not let him go. But it is a week now and Robert does not deserve this. He is only an innocent eleven-year-old boy and he needs to be back at home with us, going to school and doing the things a normal boy does. He [the abductor] is not out there by himself – I think the person who is holding Robert must have help. They must be getting extra food, extra milk, extra bread. This person who has Robert is definitely not by himself.'

Majella again renewed her plea for Robert's safe release, saying that their family was devastated without Robert. 'If someone has him, I know they have done a terrible thing but if they could just return him to us it would not be the worst scenario. Please, please just let him go – Robert is smart enough to get back home to us no matter where you let him go. He is a very intelligent boy and he has a mobile phone. He will make contact. Just let him go and bring this to an end. Please God, just bring this to an end.'

Majella also pleaded with the public to report anything suspicious, no matter how insignificant, particularly in light of the TV reconstruction of Robert's last movements which was now about to be broadcast. 'Every piece of information is vital, everything is important. The Gardaí and particularly Supt Liam Hayes have been fantastic and they are keeping our hopes up. We are being told that no news is good news and that they have not found a body. Robert is still missing and I am afraid he has gone to England or somewhere.'

It was clearly difficult for the couple having to watch someone who, from a distance, was identical to Robert doing all the things their son had done just a week earlier. But the family were deeply grateful to the Cork boy who had agreed to take part in the reconstruction and Majella, who watched part of the reconstruction from her house, specifically asked the Gardaí to pass on her thanks to the boy and his mother who had driven him to Midleton from Cork.

Not surprisingly, the reconstruction dominated every television news bulletin that night and footage of the boy replicating Robert's last known movements would be replayed throughout future coverage of the case.

WEDNESDAY, 12 JANUARY 2005
THE DISCOVERY, DAY NINE

There are some things in life you know you'll never forget. And I know that, years from now, I'll still be able to conjure up with terrible clarity the images of that bitterly cold Wednesday lunchtime when, standing outside Midleton Garda station, I was one of the first to hear that the search for Robert Holohan was about to become a hunt for his killer. What made the scene all the more surreal was that, for the first and only time in the nine-day search, the media were allowed into Midleton Garda station to film the incident room where the hunt for Robert was being co-ordinated. In a bizarre twist of fate ... in those few minutes while the photographers and TV cameramen were inside the station the news was broadcast over a live Garda radio microphone that a body had just been found at Inch strand.

For some reason, reporters had been asked to wait outside the Garda station while the photographers took their shots. We merely presumed that Supt Kevin Donohoe from the Garda Press Office was going to address us later in the day and we simply weren't needed in the incident room. However, tensions had been growing between some elements of the media and the Gardaí over the previous few days. A number of articles had been published that raised questions over the hunt for Robert. A handful of reporters felt that the Gardaí were being less than forthcoming with information and, in one case, this led to a strong exchange of views between a reporter and a Garda who stressed that their first priority was finding Robert, not providing daily copy for the media pool in East Cork. It was hard to argue with him, not least given the clear fact that Midleton Gardaí felt they had a moral duty to the Holohan family and would let nothing – particularly the media – frustrate their hunt to find Robert.

It now emerged that the Gardaí were going to issue a detailed statement about the status of their operation. In a situation where there had been little or no news about Robert for nine days, we all wondered what was the statement going to be about. Was it possible that, as some papers had speculated, the search for Robert was going to switch overseas?

These were just some of the thoughts occupying most of us as we waited patiently outside the Garda station. Then I noticed Ken Fogarty, the cameraman from TV3, emerge white-faced from the station. He gestured to Paul Byrne of TV3 and the duo immediately moved towards their jeep. I turned to them as they passed and Ken simply said: 'You won't believe this! A body has just been found at Inch. We heard it over a Garda radio mike inside.' Ken – with admirable foresight – had his own microphone switched to record throughout his time inside the station and that heartbreaking Garda radio call was the headline item on the 5.30pm TV3 news that evening.

The scene outside the Garda station instantly transformed from one of relaxed lethargy as we waited for a news release to one of total pandemonium as reporters and photographers raced to check what had happened. The sense of shock quickly dispelled and there was suddenly a frantic scramble for Inch. Privately, I was relieved that I had decided to go to the Garda station instead of waiting at the East Cork golf club. The problem now was, I didn't have a clue where Inch strand was. Luckily, Niall O'Connor of the *Irish Sun* was in the group and, being from the nearby town of Cobh he knew the way. So we sped towards the coast in convoy. And, as I ran towards my car, I spotted Supt Liam Hayes and Chief Supt Kieran McGann racing across the street. Things were obviously beginning to move at pace.

Even now, I pity anyone trying to find their way to Inch without having some knowledge of the East Cork roads. I know one reporter who got hopelessly lost and didn't arrive at Inch until well over an hour after the rest of us. The problem was complicated by the fact that there are two places called Inch in East Cork. The Inch the Gardaí were now about to seal off is located just off the Whitegate/Guileen road junction twelve miles south of Ballyedmond. I arrived together with about four other media cars just as the Gardaí were beginning to erect security tape around the isolated crossroads.

Inch strand is located down a narrow laneway off the Midleton, Whitegate and Guileen crossroads, and to the left of the laneway towards the coast lies a deep gully or ditch. The body had apparently been found down in the ditch, some thirty metres or more from the crossroads. The strand was popular with locals and with young watersports enthusiasts who favoured it because of waves suited to surfboarding and windsurfing.

Uniformed Gardaí kept the media well back from the crossroads and, over the period of the next few hours, the area became a parking hazard as Garda jeeps, forensic lab vans, television satellite trucks and reporters' cars lined the various narrow access roads. Shortly after

Leabharlanna Poibli Chathair Baile Átha Cliath
Dublin City Public Libraries

3.00pm I learned that the body had been discovered fully clothed, and the garments appeared to match those that Robert Holohan was wearing on 4 January. My sources indicated that the size of the body also appeared, at first glance, to indicate that it was a young person rather than an adult. Few of us now doubted that the search for Robert had reached an appalling, tragic finale. A short time later Fr Billy O'Donovan, Midleton curate, arrived at the scene and was ushered by Gardaí past the media and straight down to where the body was located.

A local GP had already confirmed that the boy was dead, and Fr O'Donovan now administered the last rites. Just three days earlier he had led the special prayer service at Midleton's Church of the Holy Rosary for Robert's safe return. The fleeting picture of Fr O'Donovan administering the sign of the cross to a body hidden in undergrowth, caught by a long TV lens, became one of the most dramatic images of the entire story. Shortly after 4.00pm I realised I had to get back to Midleton as I had no way of filing my stories from Inch, and it was clear that the scene was going to be preserved pending the arrival of forensic experts and the State Pathologist, Dr Marie Cassidy. And that was going to take some time.

Throughout the afternoon I'd been briefing my news desk on developments, and I knew they would take every single inch of copy I could write. Luckily, the *Irish Independent* feature writer, Gemma O'Doherty, was in Midleton that day to write a piece for the coming weekend's supplement. She was immediately diverted to Inch and I could now leave the colour writing entirely to her for tomorrow's paper. I could concentrate on the investigative dimension. My contacts had already given me a few precious hints about what was happening. The body was indeed believed to be that of Robert Holohan – and the area around Whitegate-Guileen-Inch had been targeted thanks to specific information obtained from the use of mobile phone technology. That line became the lead story for both the *Irish Independent* and *The Irish Times* the following day.

Gemma and I were also fortunate to meet one of the team of volunteers that had helped locate the body. John O'Mahony said he couldn't believe it when, after two colleagues examined an area just off the Ballycotton-Guileen junction, they spotted the remains in a ditch to the left of a pathway. 'We were searching the area really well and, as we walked down towards the strand, there was something strange down in the bushes,' he explained. 'I knew they were human all right, but I just couldn't see whether it was the body of an adult or a child. There were Gardaí and Army lads around so we knew not to go near the body so as not to damage the scene and the area.'

John and the team of volunteers had spent that morning combing woodland and scrubland around Whitegate, Inch and Guileen. They had originally searched in the Whitegate area but had been moved to Inch by late morning. Their search area now focused on land just off the access pathway from the crossroads to Inch strand. John said it was a miracle they had found the body; if it had fallen to the base of the ditch and into heavy undergrowth, there was a very real risk it might never have been found.

But the volunteers, from what they saw, believed that the body had somehow got tangled in briars and was wedged partially down the slope. The upper portion of the body's feet and legs were the first thing that the search team had seen. They appeared to have been clothed.

Back in Midleton, the sense of shock was transforming into a mounting mood of horror. Fr O'Donovan best summed up the mood: 'It's been awful for the whole community, what else can you say about something like this,' he said. Others shared that sense of pain with Mark and Majella Holohan. Former Midleton mayor, Cllr Maurice Ahern, said that hearing the news that a body had been discovered was like 'being punched in the stomach. Everyone has worked so hard and prayed so hard for this to have a happy outcome – the whole town is just numb with shock. It has touched everyone in the town – every family has reacted to this terrible disappearance.'

I had found an Internet café and the owner had kindly agreed to stay open until around 8.00pm when I explained my need to file copy. As I began writing, I was shocked to hear that Gardaí had discovered another body in a nearby river. In a day of shocks it came as a bolt from the blue; as fate would have it, this discovery was to prove totally unconnected to the tragedy at Inch. The body of the middle-aged man was recovered from the river outside Midleton town and it was later confirmed he had drowned in what appeared to have been a tragic event. The only startling connection was that, after a huge manhunt lasting nine days in Midleton, two bodies were discovered within two hours of each other. Gemma eventually joined me in the café and we compared notes and double-checked that our various stories had every pertinent detail of the discovery so far. The shock-waves were already rocketing around the community and we heard that Midleton CBS, Robert's old school, was going to stage a minute's silence the next day. And I knew that tomorrow was going to prove a very, very long day.

THURSDAY, 13 JANUARY 2005
THE LONG WAIT, DAY TEN

It was such a bitterly cold morning. The frost that had descended overnight covered every bramble, nettle and tree in sight. Every breath generated a small fog-bank that seemed to hover in the still air. The cold seemed to last even longer because the crossroads were so sheltered.

I had arrived back at Inch around 5.30am. I'd finally finished work around midnight the evening before but I knew today was going to be far more demanding. The *Evening Herald* had so far covered the story with their own Dublin-based reporters, but I knew I'd have to cover the entire Inch element of the story today. I got my first phone call at 6.30am and I was still dealing with the *Herald* at lunchtime. I said a silent prayer of thanks that I'd taken the precaution of bringing a spare, fully-charged mobile phone with me. I was certainly going to need it.

I wasn't alone in feeling under pressure. I thought I'd be the first at the scene in Inch, but how wrong I was. The two television outside broadcast vans had obviously parked here overnight, and there was already a smattering of photographers and radio reporters getting ready to file for the early-morning bulletins. Uniformed Gardaí were manning the security cordon at the crossroads and I reckoned there would also be uniformed Gardaí guarding the scene where the body still lay. The bitter cold made their job all the more difficult but, as with the search operation from the East Cork golf club, local generosity was helping to warm more than frozen limbs.

After five hours standing around the freezing crossroads, I noticed one of the reporters walking past with a breakfast roll. Hungrily, I asked him where he got it, ready to complain if he said he had gone back to Midleton without offering to get food for the rest of us. But, to my surprise, he pointed back up the road and said a woman up there was handing them out. I walked up the road and, sure enough, there were two women handing out breakfast rolls and hot drinks from the rear of a Ford Fiesta car. I explained that I wasn't a member of the emergency services, but could I possibly buy one of the rolls? The women, sisters Janet and Susan Higgins, looked slightly confused and simply told me the drinks and food were for anyone who wanted them. I again offered to pay but they politely declined. Out of curiosity, I asked them what organisation had arranged for such kindness and they replied that they lived in the area and had been horrified to hear that Robert's body was found locally. 'It was the least we could do, no one can believe that this could happen here. We just wanted to try and help those people who were helping the family,' Janet explained. She wanted to do something to show that this kind of tragedy was not what their area was all about. So she spent over €200 of her own money at a garage that morning buying breakfast rolls, tea and coffee to offer free to anyone at the crime scene as a simple gesture of support. The sisters then drove around the security zone erected around Inch strand and the Whitegate-Ballycotton junction and offered the refreshments to anyone who had been on duty all night in freezing temperatures. To this day, it remains one of the stories I tell to try and explain exactly how Midleton, in the depths of despair, managed to find an abundance of community spirit and decency.

Even the Gardaí, in the midst of such an appalling tragedy, were taken aback by the wave of kindness shown to them. One Garda accepted dozens of wreaths and fresh flower bouquets from locals, and then walked one mile from the traffic perimeter to place the flowers near an impromptu memorial to the boy. One moving tribute, from a family in Carrigtwohill, simply said: 'God needed another hurler in heaven.'

In Guileen, a local farmer bought a case of mineral water bottles and spent that morning driving around the entire perimeter of the security zone, supplying drinks to all Gardaí on duty. Many of the Gardaí were literally manning traffic checkpoints at crossroads in the middle of nowhere. As I was leaving Inch later that afternoon, I stopped about two miles from the scene to check with a lone Garda on traffic duty if he needed anything. I was stunned when he said he'd been offered more food and drinks than if he'd been on duty in Midleton or Cork. 'It's hard to believe how decent people can be,' he told me. 'This morning I've had offers of breakfast, tea, coffee, water and milk. A couple of families called down to me and said when I'm off security duty at this crossroads, I have to call up to their house for lunch or tea.'

Back at Inch, as the morning progressed the crowds continued to gather until the Gardaí eventually decided to limit access to the crossroads by closing roads some two miles away to everything except local or official traffic. One colleague who arrived at the scene at 10.00am told me he'd had to walk almost two miles to Inch from where he had parked his car. I was kept busy over the morning doing some radio interviews with Gerry Ryan on 2FM and Pat Kenny on RTÉ Radio

One. I knew Barry Roche of *The Irish Times* was doing the same with 96FM and Today FM while Jennie O'Sullivan was briefing the 'News At One'. The question everyone seemed to want to know was: Why was the body still in the ditch almost twenty-four hours after it had been discovered?

The simple answer was that the Gardaí were leaving absolutely nothing to chance and were taking every precaution that vital evidence wasn't damaged or rendered useless through rushing the processing of the scene. There was still widespread concern, particularly amongst commentators, about how the Holohan family could endure knowing that their son's body had been left lying in a freezing ditch for yet another night. We presumed that Mark and Majella might be able to see their son's remains at Cork University Hospital (CUH) or, failing that, that they would get the body back sometime on Friday. Tragically, what none of us knew then was that Mark and Majella had had their last look at their beloved son on 4 January. When they would get his coffin back on Friday it would be sealed. The last time Majella Holohan would see her son's smiling, happy face was as he disappeared out of the driveway of their home that Tuesday lunchtime, heading downhill on his beloved BMX.

Slowly, we began to get an emerging picture of what the Gardaí were now looking for. The finding on the cause of death by Dr Marie Cassidy was the crucial starting point, and any clues yielded by the analysis of the scene and the material found near the body would then focus the Garda hunt for Robert's killer. We were unlikely to get any indication of the cause of death until tomorrow (Friday) when the full post-mortem had been completed. Gardaí were already trawling through a host of details from locals. One had reported suspicious activity and a sighting of an old caravan filled with board games, a mattress and a pair of Nike runners. Another local reported seeing two vehicles: a large estate-type car and a red-coloured van being driven at high speed through the Inch area the previous Monday or Tuesday.

Both reports were treated as credible and investigated. One person, who was out walking and spotted the caravan, said that the condition and contents appeared unusual. A large bonfire was also lit on the strand not far away, though Gardaí were unclear by whom.

Gardaí were also probing suggestions that the vehicles did not have Irish licence plates, with the estate-type car having a British licence plate and the van appearing to have a Continental plate. As part of their inquiry, Gardaí also began stopping and checking all red and white vans in the general Midleton area. Gardaí also tried to eliminate three high-roofed Ford Transit or Toyota Hiace-type vans from their inquiry. All of this proceeded while uniformed officers began a pains-taking check on all homes in the area, including holiday homes which are usually left empty over the winter months.

Another Cork colleague, Ann Mooney of the *Irish Mirror*, had heard from her sources that the body, while fully clothed, had been found with some bags partially wrapped around it. There were also unconfirmed reports that Gardaí had found evidence of a fire near the scene, but the full details of this would not emerge for several days to come.

By 12.00pm the Garda technical experts had sufficiently processed the scene to allow Dr Cassidy to begin her work. Her investigation lasted from 12.35pm to 1.30pm. Just minutes after Dr Cassidy had finished, a hearse that had been waiting was signalled to the scene and Robert's body was gently placed into a polished timber coffin and removed to Cork University Hospital where a full post-mortem exami-nation would be carried out. Prayers were said as the boy's body left Inch – and, later that day, Fr Billy O'Donovan attempted to address the pain, shock and horror of the entire community at a special prayer service.

'This morning Robert doesn't need our prayers any more because we believe he is safely in the hands of God, so our prayers turn to Mark and Majella his parents, Emma and Harry, his grandparents, family, neighbours and friends,' he said. 'We pray that God may give them comfort, strength and consolation on this day and in the days ahead.' Fr O'Donovan said the horrific death of Robert was already beginning to have a huge impact on the community. One parent, he said, had told him that she could not bring up her children in the way she had intended and now had to change. 'The country was where Robert lived, where children can ride their bicycles, run freely and be exuberant like children are allowed to be. That has changed,' he said.

My colleague, Eugene Hogan, spoke to one woman after the service and I think her comment best summed up the mood in the town that had endured such an emotional roller-coaster for the previous ten days. 'What do you say? How do you explain this? Fr O'Donovan did as best he could, but words just don't work here anymore,' she said.

Gardaí also decided they had enough material to stage a formal press conference and launch an appeal for the killer to come forward. The press conference was staged just after 8.00pm in the Midleton Park hotel's ballroom and was attended by all the senior Gardaí leading the investigation: Supt Líam Hayes, Chief Supt Kieran McGann, Assistant Commissioner Tony Hickey and Supt Kevin Donohoe of the Garda Press Office. Without the full post-mortem results or the technical analysis of the scene, Gardaí were cautious as to what they ruled out. The event attracted a huge media presence and it dominated the evening news as well as the following day's newspapers. My clearest recollection emerging from the press conference was one of confusion: Where, precisely, was the investigation going? Not for the first time I got the feeling that Gardaí knew a lot more than they were saying and that a lot of the material debated during the press conference had little or no bearing on what would happen next.

Repeatedly questioned about an international dimension to the case, Gardaí confirmed that they had been liaising with police in Britain and Belgium. A central database was being used at the UK police college at Bramshill to sift through information that had already come to light during the ten-day investigation and compare it with evidence already on file. The Bramshill database had already been used by Gardaí in Operation Trace, the Garda hunt for the bodies of six women who disappeared in the Leinster region and are now presumed dead. Gardaí also said they would expand their inquiries further to the US and Canada if this was thought necessary. And yet Gardaí admitted that the scene at Inch would indicate that Robert's killer had some detailed local knowledge – something hardly likely in an opportunistic foreign killer.

The most detailed revelation of the press conference was that Gardaí were working to eliminate thirty-six people, all known sex offenders, from their inquiry. One of the most disturbing aspects of the previous ten days was the revelation of the number of convicted sex offenders who were living in the general East Cork area; many of them were not on the Sex Offenders' Register because their crimes pre-dated the list. The revelation caused outrage amongst parents and community groups, many of whom said they felt vulnerable not knowing who was living in their area. But with no idea whether there was any sexual motive behind Robert's death, Gardaí insisted they were merely keeping their investigative options open.

The impact of this fear on Midleton is hard to overstate. One of the most pointed images of the town over the previous days was the sight of normally crowded playgrounds lying empty, and virtually every child being escorted by a parent or relative. The sight of a lone, unescorted child was extremely rare in Midleton over those terrible days.

Assistant Commissioner Tony Hickey used the occasion to appeal directly to the killer: 'It would be foolish of us not to ask the killer or killers to come and see us.' He explained that in previous cases killers had expressed relief when they were arrested that they would not be able to kill again. It was confirmed that Robert would be buried on Saturday.

In light of the local mood, Supt Liam Hayes said that it was 'perfectly understandable' that a sense of fear would exist among the people of the region because of what had happened to Robert. And he vowed that Gardaí would not rest until the killer was brought to justice.

FRIDAY, 14 JANUARY 2005
THE BREAKTHROUGH, DAY ELEVEN

If twenty-four hours is a long time in politics, it can be an eternity in a criminal investigation. From the broad-based, general investigation of the evening before, the Garda probe was now direct, focused and closing in on Robert's killer. Detectives received data from Dr Cassidy and their own technical experts pointing their probe into an increasingly narrow area. There was no evidence of a sexual assault – and Garda experts believed they successfully 'lifted' fingerprint traces from the plastic found by Robert's body.

Gardaí now believed that the killer was almost certainly a local person – and senior detectives suspected that the eleven-year-old may have known his killer and died within hours of meeting him in the afternoon of 4 January. The hunt became more focused after the post-mortem examination on the body showed that Robert had been asphyxiated and had not been sexually assaulted. The latter was hugely significant because it effectively ended two important areas of Garda investigation: that Robert had been targeted by a convicted sex offender or he might have been the victim of an opportunistic killer from abroad.

While further forensic tests were still to be carried out, it was also revealed that Robert was killed while placed in an armlock. Dr Cassidy's six-hour examination revealed that Robert died through compression of the neck and windpipe, resulting in a lack of oxygen; there were no apparent ligature marks, which suggested that a cord or rope was not used. From a careful analysis of the scene at Inch, Gardaí also suspected that Robert was killed elsewhere. They now redoubled their efforts to trace vehicles that travelled the route between his home in

Ballyedmond and the cul de sac leading to the beach where the body was dumped.

The Garda theory now was that the killer panicked after the killing and put a black bin liner-type bag partially over the body before throwing it over an incline down to a marshy gully. Robert's mobile phone and one of his Nike runners were found beside the body and the badly decomposed state of the body indicated that it had probably been left there on the first afternoon of his disappearance. The body had also been damaged by wildlife and Robert's identity was confirmed through dental records only.

Two State forensic scientists who visited the scene at Inch were now assisting Dr Cassidy with further tests at a State laboratory. Robert's clothing was also being analysed for possible clues, while the Nokia 3200 phone was being examined for fingerprints and its call log being explored. Telecommunications experts examined all mobile phone traffic in the area, while Gardaí hoped that the results of toxicological and tissue-sample tests would answer further questions.

Whereas Gardaí were cautious at the press conference the previous evening and were keeping their options open, senior officers were now visibly confident of a breakthrough. Supt Liam Hayes said they were pleased with the evidential material now coming through. 'We are very hopeful of bringing Robert's killer to justice. But we cannot say any more at this stage,' he said. The initial medical findings also indicated that the killer was likely to have had significant upper body strength.

More than a hundred calls were made to Gardaí following that televised press conference and officers were again working on eliminating vehicles from their inquiries. These included a white pick-up truck that was seen unattended with a door open about a hundred yards from the Holohan home, a silver Volvo car, a black jeep and three white vans, one with red stripes. Gardaí were anxious to contact a well-dressed man who had been seen walking in Egan's and Staunton's fields near where Robert was last seen alive.

I wasn't alone amongst the reporters on duty in thinking that these questions, once central to the investigation, were now mere shadow-boxing compared to the lab work that was progressing. Gardaí had a scene to process, they had great hopes of technical experts uncovering major clues and a realistic hope of identifying the killer as a result.

But the geographic search operation around East Cork continued, albeit on a much smaller scale. The Gardaí search effort was again supported by the Defence Forces with over eighty-five Army personnel drawn from Limerick, Cork and Kilkenny. Commandant Dan Harvey of the Southern Brigade said that the army would continue to make itself available to Gardaí for as long as was required. Commandant Harvey explained: 'We have one team deployed here at the crime scene and we are searching in a radial pattern outwards along the road-ways. The other team is deployed in Ballyspillane, just east of the Bal-lyedmond area near the home.

'We have been deployed in areas with particularly rough terrain that require more disciplined methodology than can be given by civilian search teams. With each team, we have four Gardaí and they are effec-tively leading the searches. Items such as machetes, bill hooks and metal detectors are all being used in the search in a bid to glean even a speck of evidence. For instance, our Vallon metal detectors are sensi-tive up to a depth of eighteen inches, so if there is anything out there of evidential value in the areas we are searching, then we are likely to get it,' he said.

And then, poignantly, came the moment that everyone had dreaded for so very long – the return of Robert's body to Ballyedmond and his parents, Mark and Majella. Shortly after lunch, Robert's body was released back to the care of his family and a hearse from T. Wallis undertakers brought it, complete with Garda escort, the twelve miles or so from CUH back to Ballyedmond. We had learned earlier that after-noon that Robert was going to have a private wake in his home attended by family, close friends and immediate neighbours. Such was the discretion at the removal that hardly any photographs were taken of the hearse on that tragic journey.

Robert's funeral would take place at 3.00pm in Midleton's Church of the Holy Rosary. As I headed home that evening, I talked with Jennie O'Sullivan from RTÉ and Barry Roche from *The Irish Times*. We all believed that Gardaí felt an arrest was now only a matter of time. And, judging by previous cases, an arrest would be highly unlikely on the day of Robert's funeral.

CHAPTER 4: THE FUNERAL

SATURDAY, 15 JANUARY 2005
THE FUNERAL, DAY TWELVE

Midleton is a prosperous town, a traditional Irish farmers' market town too far from Cork city to be a mere suburb, yet close enough that it can attract commuters. Its bustling main street is proof of the thriving nature of the East Cork capital. Packed with shops, restaurants and pubs, the town's main street is like a window into modern Ireland: busy, wealthy and brash. For centuries, the farmland around had been regarded as some of the richest in Ireland. The town was the traditional home to Ireland's whiskey industry and its Jameson Whiskey Heritage Centre is one of Cork's main tourist attractions.

Times were good in East Cork and most traders knew it. There was even talk that the local railway line, closed over forty years before, would re-open to cater for the flood of commuters quitting nearby Cork city for the quieter life in the country town.

But yet, despite the fact that the Christmas lights and decorations were still hanging in some business premises on that bright winter afternoon, this was to be a very different kind of day.

At lunchtime, one by one, the Midleton shop premises began to close their doors. Some placed black ribbons on their doorways before turning off the lights and closing the shutters. Pubs that would normally be thronged with shopping-weary husbands were empty and silent. The streets were crowded but almost everyone seemed to be hurrying elsewhere. By 3.00pm, only one shop in Midleton was still open – the German supermarket, Lidl.

Yet the only outward sign that something was amiss came from the lines of Garda traffic cones that stretched for over a hundred metres from the main street right beyond Midleton's Church of the Holy Rosary. Today, Robert Holohan would be buried and an entire community would grieve.

Just two miles north of the town, Mark and Majella Holohan were desperately trying to prepare themselves for the agony that lay ahead. Just twenty-four hours before, their eldest son was finally returned to them eleven days after he disappeared. Robert's return was the stuff of every parent's nightmare. The hearse drew up outside their dormer bungalow in Ballyedmond complete with Garda escort, and the small white coffin in the back seemed totally undersized.

For two days, their boy's remains had been the focus of one of the most intensive Garda technical and forensic examinations ever conducted. Such was the painstaking nature of the investigation that Robert's body – to the horror of his parents – was left lying in the ditch at Inch strand overnight to ensure that no evidence was missed or accidentally destroyed.

When the body was finally moved at lunchtime it wasn't to be brought home, instead it was transferred to the morgue at CUH for a full post-mortem examination by State Pathologist, Dr Marie Cassidy. And when Robert finally returned to Ballyedmond shortly after lunch on 14 January , the small white coffin was sealed – and Mark and Majella were urged not to open it because of animal damage suffered by their son's body.

The only tangible contact they had left with their handsome eldest son was a lock of his golden blond hair that was handed to them by an ashen-faced Garda. In the circumstances, the Holohans decided to offer Robert a traditional 'wake' in his home. Friends, family and neighbours gathered that Friday night to try and support Mark and Majella, and put some sense on the tragic killing of a young boy.

Amongst the most devastated of the mourners present was Wayne O'Donoghue, the Holohans' next-door-neighbour and a young man regarded by many, including Mark and Majella, as the older brother Robert never had. Wayne appeared to have taken Robert's disappearance particularly hard. His girlfriend, Rebecca Dennehy, noted that he was much quieter than normal. She felt that he was blaming himself for Robert's disappearance having refused to take him to town earlier on the day he disappeared. The Holohans were so grateful for all that Wayne had done during the huge search effort that they wanted him to say a Prayer of the Faithful at their son's Requiem Mass.

Gardaí gently and carefully suggested that Cork GAA star, Seán Óg Ó hAilpín, might be asked instead. The hurling star agreed and delayed his departure for a sports tour of New Zealand so that he could support the family during the funeral. Ó hAilpín had issued a personal appeal for information on Robert's whereabouts twenty-four hours after the boy went missing after learning that the boy idolised him. His involvement also brought hundreds of search volunteers from the GAA. Ó hAilpín had even visited the Holohans' home at Ballyedmond to express his personal support during their ordeal. But what only a handful of senior Gardaí knew was that they preferred Ó hAilpín to perform the Church reading because Wayne O'Donoghue was already the prime suspect in Robert's killing.

At noon, Midleton parish church began to fill, even though there were still three hours to the scheduled start of Robert's Requiem Mass. The large church has ample capacity for more than 2000. Today, the church would cope with over 4000 – over 2000 of whom had to queue outside, unable to get into the church. Such were the crowds that one woman fainted and had to be helped out. One hour before the service began, the sound of sobs rang audibly around the church interior.

Those who knew Robert were easily identified by the anguished looks on their faces.

The church interior itself was a sea of flowers and wreaths – some with heart-rending messages such as 'Goodbye, God's newest angel' or 'God needed a new hurler in heaven'. The black-and-white Midleton GAA colours that Robert wore so proudly were everywhere to be seen, mostly worn by his former classmates. The children from the GAA club and Midleton CBS, who were to form a guard of honour for Robert's last journey, looked nervous and uncertain – as if as this was nothing more than a bad dream.

The tear-stained faces of their parents mingled with the uniforms of Ireland's emergency services: the Gardaí, the Army, the Naval Service, the Irish Coastguard, the Civil Defence and Midleton Fire Brigade. Equally prominent were the formal insignia of officials from East Cork Golf Club, Midleton GAA and a host of other local organisations.

Cmdt Michael Murray represented An Taoiseach, Bertie Ahern, as his Aide-de-Camp, while Col Ray King represented President Mary McAleese. The Cabinet was represented both by Micheál Martin, Minister for Trade, Enterprise and Employment, and Children's Minister Brian Lenihan. Local politicians, Minister Michael Ahern and David Stanton TD, both of whom had taken part in the search effort, led a strong local political presence including Cork's County Mayor, Cllr Paddy Sheehan and Cork's Deputy Lord Mayor, Cllr Mary Shields. Midleton's Mayor, Cllr Ted Murphy, led the Town Council delegation while official Brendan Barry represented Midleton Traders' Association. It was Brendan who had helped co-ordinate the incredible gesture where every shop in Midleton, with just one exception, had closed for the duration of the funeral.

Midleton curate Fr O'Donovan assured the hushed crowd, as the Requiem Mass began, that Robert Holohan would have revelled in all the attention. 'Robert loved being the star of the show – and he is the star of the show here today,' Fr O'Donovan explained.

The service included a special message from President Mary McAleese – who said the suffering of the Holohan family and the Midleton community had touched every heart in Ireland. 'The community goodness and support has won the hearts of the people of Ireland. Midleton has responded with resilience, dignity and sheer goodness. The stranger has become a neighbour.'

Yet there was no hiding the abject, awful grief of Mark and Majella. Solidarity and dignity are wonderful virtues, but scant consolation for parents who are mourning a dead child.

The Requiem Mass finally began with Mark and a sobbing Majella escorting their son's white coffin down the central aisle. The Bishop of Cloyne, Dr John Magee, had insisted on personally attending the service together with Fr O'Donovan and eighteen other members of the Midleton and East Cork clergy. Supt Liam Hayes, who was leading the hunt for Robert's killer, was also with the family for support as were some of the most senior Gardaí in the State. Members of the elite Garda NBCI also attended the service, but their interest lay in a dark-haired young man who was also in the church. While every other eye in Midleton church rested on the suffering Mark and Majella Holohan, several NBCI detectives stayed calmly focused on Wayne O'Donoghue.

Fr O'Donovan assured the assembled crowd that the anguish of the Holohans at the appalling loss of their son would be eased by the incredible scenes of solidarity and sympathy within Midleton and its surrounding areas. 'They have the support and prayers of the nation … Mark and Majella will start the long journey of coping with their grief and in time of putting their lives back together again. They will do this with the bravery, courage and dignity they have shown throughout this ordeal,' he added.

The sense of tragedy was poignantly underpinned by a simple story of how one Garda, assigned to protect Robert's body while it lay overnight in the Inch ditch just forty-eight hours previously, had felt such pity at what the boy had endured that he spent the night talking to the body. 'I just wanted him to know that he wasn't alone,' the congregation heard.

Standing, pressed like a sardine at the back of the Church, I remember thinking that the service was so moving that everyone would be left emotionally drained. To my left, a young woman was sobbing, head bowed, a friend's arm wrapped around her shoulders. Beside me, a tall, bearded man was leaning back against the limestone pillars, eyes closed, and tears silently trickling down his cheeks.

Then the Bishop of Cloyne, Dr John Magee, moved forward and addressed the congregation. He spoke of hurt, he spoke of community support but, crucially, he spoke directly to Robert's killer. 'May the one who has been responsible for this heinous crime against an innocent child come forward and face up to the responsibilities incurred. And he can then repay the debt to society that is owed and seek the mercy and forgiveness from an all-merciful God.'

Dr Magee was full of praise for the community support shown towards the Holohan family in their time of suffering and for the incredible work by the Gardaí in trying to bring young Robert home to his family. The former secretary to three pontiffs also thanked Midleton curate, Fr O'Donovan, for the Trojan work he had performed in supporting the Holohan family, in helping address community grief and for leading the church's response to the terrible tragedy. Fittingly, when Dr Magee delivered his tribute to Fr O'Donovan, spontaneous applause immediately erupted throughout the church, and a special 'thank you' from Robert's parents was privately said to Fr O'Donovan afterwards.

Finally, the service drew to a close. For many, it was a physically and emotionally exhausting day. Friends and family of the Holohans waited nervously as Mark and Majella prepared for undoubtedly the hardest walk of their lives – the 200 metre trek down the church and through the adjoining cemetery to where Robert would be laid to rest.

As the cortège finally began to move, Majella Holohan leaned forward and gently embraced the sealed white coffin that contained her son. She stroked the coffin as if in compensation for being prevented from hugging her son one final time. Mark Holohan took up position to the front, guiding his son on his final journey as he had guided him so many times out fishing, playing hurling and kicking a ball around their garden.

The scenes outside the church almost beggared belief. Over two thousand people stood packed into the churchyard and cemetery. Slowly, the cortège wound its way through the graveyard to the Holohan plot. The grave was already piled high with wreaths, flowers, toys and mementoes. One child had placed a teddy by the plot with the simple note: 'For Robert'. A family friend, familiar with Robert's love of horses, had placed a plastic horse by the plot. A photo of Robert's beloved horse, Stella, rested nearby.

Friends would later say that the graveside was the hardest part of all for both Mark and Majella. With Robert's body having already lain in a freezing ditch for almost nine days, it must have seemed too cruel for his parents to see Robert's remains again confined to the cold embrace of the earth.

Fifteen minutes later, the ceremony was finally over. The crowds began to drift away and the Holohans were left to retreat to their private anguish. A few friends formed a cordon around the couple as if to try and protect them from the assembled media and onlookers. A Garda liaison officer stayed with the family for the entire day offering them support and updates on the hunt for their son's killer.

That Saturday night would be remembered as one of the longest of Majella Holohan's life, and yet the couple had to try desperately to maintain a façade of normality for the sake of their other two children. Robert's younger brother had been waking over the previous few nights, crying out for his brother to come home. He couldn't understand why Robert was gone – and, his heartbroken parents said, he wanted his big brother back. Yet any shred of normality that might have been left in Midleton after the trauma of Robert's killing was about to be dramatically shattered.

Gardaí now had firm evidence linking a suspect to the scene at Inch strand where Robert's body had been found. Virtually every reporter in Midleton knew that nothing was likely to happen on the day of the funeral – any major developments were likely to come tomorrow.

Above: Robert Holohan, pictured during a family holiday abroad.

Below: The photo of Robert that was used during the search.

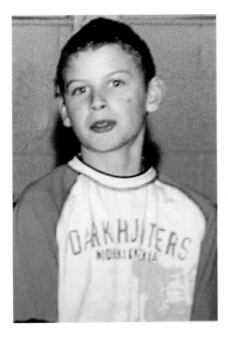

Above: Gardaí searching the mile-long road where Robert's bike was found.

Below: The search continues in Midleton.

Above: Members of the army searching the area around the Holohan family home (in the background).

Below: Assistant Commissioner, Tony Hickey and Chief Supt Kieran McGann pictured at the murder investigation press conference in the Midleton Park Hotel.

Above: Chief Supt Kieran McGann pictured at the murder investigation press conference in the Midleton Park Hotel.

Below: Wayne O'Donoghue during the search operation.

Right: Members of the Army searching the Midleton area for Robert.

Below: An actor poses as Robert Holohan during a reconstruction of the last known movements of the Midleton schoolboy.

Above: Majella Holohan in Robert's bedroom.

Below: The scene near Inch Cross, where Robert's body was found.

Above: Father O'Donovan and members of the Garda Síochána saying prayers beside the body of Robert Holohan at Inch strand, 12 January 2005.

The scene near to where
Robert's body was found.

CHAPTER 5: THE ARREST

SUNDAY, 16 JANUARY 2005
THE ARREST, DAY THIRTEEN

Sometimes it's the small things you remember about specific days. That Sunday, I remember being so grateful for just being able to sleep until 10.00am. The previous twelve days had been exhausting and I was glad of the late start. As I knew it would, the funeral the previous day had proved a long, arduous fourteen hours of making sure every inch of the ceremony and ongoing investigation was covered for the *Sunday Independent*.

But it was an emotionally trying day for everyone involved. Over the course of the previous days, I think all the search volunteers, Gardaí and reporters realised what truly decent, honourable people the Holohans were – a couple caught up in every parent's worst nightmare. No one had dreamed the search for Robert would end this way. Worse still, how could anyone even express gratitude that, at the very least, the family had got their son's body back. I have three children of my own and it's hard at times to ignore your own emotions – even if you are doing your job. During Robert's funeral Mass I remembered looking over at one reporter and seeing that she was crying too. Earlier in the week, my bosses, Paul Dunne and Dave Halloran, had assigned a number of other reporters to Midleton to help with the scale of the emerging story. Over the following days, I was relieved and thankful to have colleagues like Eugene Hogan, Helen Bruce and Maeve Sheehan work alongside me.

Such was the emotion in Midleton that day that Lidl quickly placed a notice in their store window apologising for any offence caused; they also wrote to Mark and Majella Holohan to express their sympathies on their tragic loss. It was just one of many aspects of the case swirling around Midleton that Sunday.

When I arrived in Midleton about 11.00am I began to scan the Sunday papers over a coffee in the Midleton Park hotel and I realised that we had, along with Shane Phelan of Sunday's *Irish Star*, one of the key breaking elements of the story – the revelation that Gardaí now had fingerprints from the scene at Inch.

But, if I was tired, what about the Gardaí, the search volunteers and the Holohan family themselves? How on earth were they managing to cope with the workload and the emotional trauma involved? But the simple fact is that the Gardaí weren't just coping – they were progressing with their manhunt to the point where a breakthrough was imminent. While bringing my coffee and papers back to the room that the hotel had kindly let the reporters use, I met Assistant Commissioner Tony Hickey of the NBCI walking along the corridor. We stopped for a brief chat about the Requiem Mass the previous day. The Assistant Commissioner ranked as one of the most experienced investigators on the force, and he had been associated with some of the biggest Garda operations of modern times. His NBCI team were a crucial cog in the entire investigation – and now, with a crime scene being processed, would bring their considerable criminal investigative skills to bear.

As we parted and I walked back to the reporters' room, I got the firm sense that something was going to happen. And I reckoned it was going to happen within the next twenty-four to forty-eight hours. In the meantime, there was plenty of work to do.

That whole afternoon was spent revising all the reports from the funeral the previous day for Monday's *Irish Independent*. These were augmented by emerging details of the Garda investigation and the fact that search teams were still operating in the general Whitegate area. Now there seemed to be a flood of data: Bishop Magee's plea to the killer to come forward; the escalating mood of outrage within Midleton; the emotional fall-out from the funeral, the awful plight of the Holohan family. But most of all, who was the killer and precisely how close were Gardaí to making their move?

I felt the key ingredient was the fingerprints. The Garda forensic and technical experts had been processing the scene at Inch since late on 12 January, four days earlier. While there was still speculation in some papers about overseas child sex offenders, the clear understanding from Gardaí I spoke to was that Midleton itself was now the area firmly under scrutiny.

Locals too felt that the investigation was accelerating, particularly when it emerged on Friday, 14 January, that Gardaí had asked for so-called 'elimination samples' of fingerprints from a number of people in the area. This was routine – but, in the space of a few hours, would prove absolutely crucial to the Garda probe.

I don't think any of the reporters covering the story had any doubt that the Gardaí suspected they knew who killed Robert. The question was, when would they move to make an arrest? By 6.00pm, we'd filed about a dozen stories in total and the only thing remaining was the page-one lead story. That wouldn't be written for a couple of hours yet – better to wait and see what developments would occur overnight. I'd already learned from one Garda source that there were concerns that the individual involved in Robert's death might be showing signs of strain and wilting under the undeniable emotional pressures involved.

The Gardaí were clearly worried that whoever had killed Robert might attempt to harm themselves either from remorse or fear of being caught. That was something that officers were very discreetly urging people in the town to bear in mind. Gardaí wanted to know about anyone who seemed under unusual or inexplicable pressure, and particularly anyone who seemed to be behaving in an odd or out-of-character fashion over recent days.

As I left the hotel to go and meet a contact down town, I bumped into my counterpart from *The Irish Times*, Barry Roche. A good friend, Barry had worked for over twenty years as a reporter in Cork. He had been covering the Robert Holohan story from the very beginning and, like myself, now felt that senior detectives knew an awful lot more than they were prepared to say at this point.

By early evening, we had filed all our stories except the front-page piece. I decided to head home for about an hour to see my three kids and, at 7.30pm, was about to head back to Midleton when Barry rang to ask had I heard anything. I said no, that I hadn't checked with my contacts since late afternoon but planned to make some calls at 8.00pm when I was back in Midleton.

Barry reckoned that something was in the air. I immediately tried to ring two of my contacts and couldn't get through to either of them. That immediately got me worried and I decided that the best place to be was outside Midleton Garda station. If there was going to be a development like an arrest, this was where it was all going to happen. I couldn't imagine for a second that if someone was taken into custody in connection with Robert's death that they would be taken to any other Garda station. Barry was already there when I arrived. Over the next hour, a number of phone calls confirmed that Gardaí were indeed poised to make an arrest.

While we both then tried to make ourselves as unobtrusive as possible, within an hour the number of reporters and photographers gathering outside the station made it clear that either the rumour-mill was working overtime or there was, indeed, something genuinely about to happen.

In Dublin, my colleague Tom Brady, the *Irish Independent*'s long-serving security correspondent, was liaising with his contacts and, just before 9.00pm, he rang me to say that a suspect was *en route* to the Garda station with arresting officers. The crowd outside had become a scrum. In fact, such was the quantity of TV camera lights and photographers' flashes that I reckoned the street lights weren't even needed. The layout of Midleton Garda station meant that the Garda car bringing the suspect could only use a single access road – and the station itself is located directly behind Midleton courthouse.

Within minutes of Tom's call, a Toyota saloon car swung round the corner and deftly whipped into the car-park. In a flurry of flash photography, two detectives escorted a man through the side door of the station. The man was wearing a heavy jacket with a baseball cap pulled low over his eyes. He didn't turn to look at the cameras on the street – and his face was effectively out of sight because of the cap. The Gardaí had made an arrest! The prime suspect for the killing of Robert Holohan was now in custody. The only questions that remained was whether there would be a charge and who the suspect was. The time constraints were such that I hadn't time to type up my story on a laptop, it had to be phoned through immediately to the newsroom in Dublin. After filing my copy, I walked back to the Garda station and, over the next hour, we gathered that the person in custody was a twenty-year-old, came from the local area and was understood to have known Robert. But what took all of us by surprise was the indication that the individual had also taken part in the search effort.

MONDAY, 17 JANUARY 2005
THE CHARGE, DAY FOURTEEN

If Sunday had been mild, Mother Nature decided to teach us a lesson that Monday evening. While the cold wasn't as severe as the numbing frost that marked that early morning at Inch on 13 January, it made the long wait for details of a court appearance extremely difficult. It was freezing cold and, as if that wasn't enough, intermittent showers fell as the afternoon turned into evening. There was little sign of any news.

Throughout the day, a throng of reporters waited outside the Garda station and Midleton courthouse for details of the formal charge. By now, we'd made enough phone calls to enough Gardaí to know that something was very likely to happen that evening – precisely when remained to be seen. Yet throughout the day, people would come and ask us precisely what was going on? The mood in the town had swung from one of fear that a killer was still on the loose to one of anger that anyone from the community could have been involved in Robert's death.

I found that while parents and families were finally relieved at the Garda breakthrough, there was widespread shock and disappointment that the man arrested was from the Midleton area. One man I spoke to on the main street said he was stunned. 'What else can you say? It is like another tragedy being inflicted on the town,' Flan Donnelly explained. 'No one around here knows what to think. There's been so many rumours, so much news, that I think we're all in a state of shock still. No one knows what to think.'

For others, like Midleton Mayor Cllr Ted Murphy, the prospect of justice being done offered hope that the town – like the Holohan family – might finally get closure on the tragedy. 'It's been a terrible time for the town and for the Holohan family. But this is a great town and these are fantastic people. We'll all get through this in time,' he insisted. But for others, the news of an arrest brought relief. 'I'm just so glad that the Garda investigation is going well. The Bishop's appeal meant a lot to people here and I hope that everyone can now start getting on with their lives,' said Mary-Kate Dwane. 'Last week we were afraid to let our children walk to school because we thought a paedophile was on the loose. Now everyone is saying that it's a tragic accident. All I want is for everyone to be able to put this behind them and get on with their lives. But I know it will be hard for the Holohans without Robert.'

Midleton Canon Bertie Troy said he felt the tragedy had brought many people to the Church seeking support and solace. 'I don't think I've ever seen so many young people at Mass.' One of the things that I noticed that Monday was the number of votive candles burning in the Church of the Holy Rosary.

But not everyone was quite so understanding or forgiving. Some locals were visibly angry that anyone from the area could have been involved in Robert's death and the disposal of his body. From 11.45pm on Sunday night, after the twenty-year-old suspect was arrested, locals had gathered outside Midleton Garda station to ask the assembled media for information or to vent their anger. 'It's a disaster – how could anyone from the town do this? How could anyone stay quiet while thousands of us were out searching in the wind and rain and looking for Robert?' one irate man asked.

As we waited for news of a court appearance, it emerged that the Garda probe was escalating. In Ballyedmond, access had been severely restricted from the previous evening by Gardaí. One contact confirmed to me that a house in the area was being examined in detail by forensic experts. So it appeared that the indication from the previous evening about the individual in custody being known to Robert was correct.

By 8.00pm there was a large crowd gathered outside the side street that linked the Garda station to the courthouse. The vast majority were reporters, photographers or TV crews. Such was the level of interest in the arrest that RTÉ, TV3 and TG4 crews were now joined by SKY and BBC crews. Mixed amongst the media were a number of local onlookers, most of whom were simply curious – but a few were clearly intent on making their feelings known to the individual under arrest.

Shortly after 8.00pm, I got a tip that the court appearance would happen shortly. After alerting my desk, I spotted North Cork District Court Judge, Michael Pattwell, arriving at the courthouse. I reckoned that it was better to secure a decent seat in the court than a glimpse of the defendant as he was led the brief walk from the side door of the station to the rear door of the courthouse. So I strolled around to the locked front door of the court and waited. A few minutes later, the court caretaker opened up, and solicitor Frank Buttimer was ushered inside. (Ironically, I had only bumped into Frank earlier that month with our respective children in tow at the Everyman Palace Christmas pantomime – but this was going to be a totally different kind of show.)

After several minutes – by now the media queue outside the front door had turned into a mob – the door opened and we were able to scramble for seats on the press bench. As I strode into the court room, I noticed that a number of people were already present, including several Gardaí who sat on the right-hand side of the room, a young man, shoulders stooped and head bowed, between them. I recognised one of the Gardaí as Midleton detective, Sergeant Brian Goulding. I didn't recognise the young man, but I had just set eyes on Wayne O'Donoghue for the first time. Later we would learn that he was Robert Holohan's next-door neighbour.

In the months to follow, several other reporters echoed what was my instant first impression – that he was such a handsome lad. I remember thinking: What on earth could have happened for him to be involved in this? The young man kept his head studiously bowed and made no eye contact with anyone. In the front row of the public gallery at the rear of the court, sat a man in a suit looking grey-faced, with a woman beside him. It appeared as if she had been crying. Later, I was to learn that these were Wayne's father, Ray, and his mother, Therese. Robert's parents, Mark and Majella, were not in Court though we learned that a family friend was watching the proceedings on their behalf. After waiting less than five minutes, Judge Michael Pattwell entered the courtroom and the hearing began. Just eight minutes later it was all over.

Detective Sergeant Brian Goulding told the Court that he had arrested O'Donoghue at 7.16pm at Oliver Plunkett Place, Midleton, and formally charged him, under Section 4 of the Criminal Law Act, with the unlawful killing of Robert Holohan at Ballyedmond,

Midleton, on 4 January last. It was a manslaughter charge and not a murder charge, as many had speculated. When charged, the defendant simply replied to Gardaí: 'I have nothing to say.' Wayne O'Donoghue appeared in Court impeccably dressed in a charcoal grey suit, a white shirt and black-and-blue striped tie. For the duration of the eight-minute hearing he kept his head bowed – only to look up on a number of brief occasions at his parents sitting opposite him in the front row.

O'Donoghue made no comment during the hearing – which was marked by a strong Garda presence in and around the courthouse. Around seventy members of the public – most in their teens and early twenties – packed the public galleries. Frank Buttimer, O'Donoghue's defence solicitor, explained that the arrest followed a lengthy voluntary interview with the Gardaí, which was arranged by an O'Donoghue family member early on Sunday afternoon.

This was followed by a Section 4 detention which commenced at 11.30pm on Sunday evening. He explained this was preceded by the earlier communication between the defendant's family and the Gardaí at 11.30am on Sunday. 'That communication at 11.30am resulted in an invitation by the accused to a member of An Garda Siochána to attend his home. He agreed to submit to a voluntary process of interview in relation to the subject of this investigation,' Mr Buttimer explained.

Supt Liam Hayes pointed out that the initial voluntary interview with Gardaí was not conducted with O'Donoghue in custody – a point that Mr Buttimer confirmed to Judge Pattwell. Supt Hayes also said that the State would be applying for O'Donoghue to be remanded in custody until the Thursday, 20 January sitting of Midleton District Court.

Mr Buttimer told the Court that his client had instructed him not to apply for bail at the current time – though he would be reserving his future position on the matter. 'He was entirely appraised of his entitlements,' Mr Buttimer confirmed. He further pointed out to the Court that his client was a twenty-year-old college student – and asked that he be remanded to Cork Prison rather than St Patrick's Institute in Dublin, given the special circumstances of the case. Judge Pattwell agreed once he was assured by Supt Hayes that proper facilities were available within Cork Prison to remand the twenty-year-old. Wayne O'Donoghue, a former Midleton secondary school student, was now a second-year engineering student at Cork Institute of Technology (CIT).

And suddenly it was all over. As the defendant was led away, there was a race for the door and TV crews tried to make their main evening broadcasts with live reports of the court hearing. Newspaper reporters rang their desks with the charge and court details. There was still a large crowd milling around outside the Court. Ted McCarthy and Darragh McSweeney, photographers with the Cork agency, Provision, told me that as O'Donoghue was being led between the Garda station and the courthouse several members of the public had shouted abuse at him. But those gathered outside the court now simply wanted to know what had happened and who was in custody. As the identity of the defendant became known, there was a visible rush back to pubs along the main street with the news.

TUESDAY, 18 JANUARY 2005
THE AFTERMATH, DAY FIFTEEN

Midleton was truly appalled by the news. Every single person I spoke to linked the horror of what the Holohans had gone through with what the O'Donoghue family must now be going through. No one expected that the horror at the killing could get worse. But it just had. The person charged with killing Robert Holohan was not a faceless stranger – in fact, he was his neighbour. Wayne O'Donoghue was popular and well known in the town. Many locals knew him from his part-time job at the Goose's Acre pub in Midleton. The O'Donoghue family was well known and respected in East Cork. Wayne's father,

Ray, operated a car sales business in Cobh while his mother, Therese, was a scion of a successful business family in nearby Castlemartyr. The fact that it was their son who had been arrested in connection with Robert Holohan's death had added shock to the overwhelming sense of tragedy that gripped the community.

Sadly, the O'Donoghues' problems were only beginning. We learned later that day that their son had had to be transferred from Cork Prison to the Midlands Prison for his own safety. The Irish Prison Service confirmed the transfer, but did not specify a reason. However, I learned from my sources that there were major concerns over the young man's safety given a number of threats levelled against him from other Cork inmates. The killing of Robert Holohan had attracted huge publicity in Cork – and obviously had generated extremely high emotions amongst the Cork Prison population. It didn't help matters that prison officials were working in Cork at a jail that was handling almost three times the number of inmates for which it had been designed.

Not surprisingly, it was decided to transfer Wayne O'Donoghue to the Midlands Prison in County Laois where it was felt he would be better accommodated. In future, all his Court appearances would involve time-consuming transfers to East Cork from Laois. And there would be quite a number of those remand appearances, six in all over the next four months.

CHAPTER 6: THE TRIAL, days 1-3

TUESDAY, 29 NOVEMBER 2005
THE TRIAL, DAY ONE

Murder trials are truly terrible experiences. Even those on the fringes of the case are left emotionally drained by the sheer pain, suffering and outrage that generally marks such hearings. But staging a high-profile trial over the killing of an eleven-year-old boy amid the lights and festive atmosphere in the lead-up to Christmas was hard to bear. Yet that is precisely what Mark and Majella Holohan endured.

Many had presumed that the Holohan case would be the first held in Cork's lavishly refurbished courthouse on Washington Street. The last murder case held in the old Cork courthouse was in early 1920 when Crown law applied and the Leeside was yet to experience the bitter fall-out of the War of Independence and the burning of the city centre by the Black and Tans. But, as it transpired, a delay in the case ensured that the first murder trial held in the city in eighty-five years was, in fact, that of a stabbing that occurred on Cork's north side. It was concluded in early November, leaving Wayne O'Donoghue to be formally arraigned before the Central Criminal Court and Cork courthouse on Tuesday, 29 November, for a trial expected to last three weeks.

As the criminal arm of the High Court moved to the Washington Street courthouse for the second time in the space of a month, even the

€26 million refurbishment of the magnificent building couldn't mask the mounting sense of tragedy and gloom surrounding the Holohan case.

As I walked into the imposing court complex early that morning, determined to secure an early place in the press gallery, I remember thinking that there was something truly surreal about that dark November day: it had been a long, long search for the boy – how on earth had it all come to this? It was hard to believe. Over one hundred jury-panel members gathered in Courtroom No. 2, sandwiched between a huge media and Garda presence. Given the high-profile nature of the case, the Court Service had ensured a large jury panel was available in case a significant number of people exempted themselves.

It is common in such criminal cases for a number of jury-panel members to seek to exempt themselves for reasons which can vary from living in the area involved (in this case Midleton) or knowing some of the principals in the proceedings, either with the defence or prosecution. If a significant number of jury-panel members seek to excuse themselves, this can cause problems, not least by reducing the number of potential jurors to hear the case. Hence, a large jury-panel pool is often essential to ensure that a case proceeds smoothly to trial.

Both the State and the defence have a specific number of objections which can be made to any jury-panel member without explanation to the Court. But an unlimited number of jury-panel members can be objected to once a specific reason is given. As it happens, a number of previous criminal cases in Cork had been heard by twelve-member juries comprised of seven men and five women; as it later transpired for the O'Donoghue trial, that ratio would be reversed, with seven women and five men. The jury foreperson was a woman.

Everyone – including the media – was nervous, as this was the most important criminal case staged in Cork for over a generation. There was simply no margin for error. Yet, outside the court, the Christmas lights twinkled and Washington Street was a hubbub of shoppers and revellers, all going about their festive tasks, seemingly oblivious to the tragedy about to unfold just yards from them.

The only sign that something unusual was underway in Cork that morning was the throng of photographers, TV crews and reporters huddled outside the Washington Inn, a premises ideally placed for monitoring both entrances to the courthouse. Such was the inclement weather that most wore weather-proof jackets and warm, woollen hats. Others sat in the Liberty Grill for a last cup of coffee before proceedings began.

Inside the court, the atmosphere was tense and expectant. The Court Service, aware that there was likely to be huge media interest in the trial, had set aside larger than normal areas for reporters. But, despite this provision, reporters ended up squeezed in beside Gardaí in the main body of the courtroom while other late-comers were forced to seek a seat in the public gallery to the rear of the court. The *Irish Examiner*, which would run three pages on proceedings each day throughout the trial, even had sketch artists to the rear of the press box to try and capture the mood for its readers. The paper's coverage of the case would be led by their experienced court correspondent, Liam Heylin, who, at various times, would have up to six colleagues working alongside him. Never before in modern times had a Cork criminal trial attracted such media coverage, and it was the first time in living memory that sketch artists had been involved. Few doubted that this was a media event like none other in Cork.

Like the rest of the Cork press corps, I was to follow the case for its duration. I had to cover for the *Irish Independent* and, for just the opening day, the *Evening Herald* as well. After that, the *Herald* would be covered by Mark Hilliard, a reporter down from Dublin for the next three weeks. This was a huge relief to me because I knew from previous experience that it is exceptionally difficult to leave a trial for thirty or forty minutes in the morning to file for an evening newspaper and then return to try and catch up on the material you've just missed for the daily paper. Better still, the *Independent* had also assigned Kathy Donaghy for colour writing for the duration of the trial. So all I had to concentrate on was straight news coverage – and, of course, securing a seat in a courtroom that, at one point, appeared to have more reporters and photographers than jury-panel members.

Minutes before the case opened, there was a hush in the room as Mark and Majella Holohan, flanked by Midleton Gardaí, made their way into the court. Mark was wearing a sombre blue suit while Majella wore a black trouser suit covered by a warm tan coat. She smiled at some faces she recognised in the crowd before the duo took seats in the main body of the courtroom, to the right and in front of the raised dais where the young man accused of their son's killing sat motionless.

*

Wayne O'Donoghue wore a charcoal suit, a white shirt and a blue-grey tie. He sat, hunched forward, his eyes fixed on the ground between his feet. His hands were gripped tightly, the knuckles almost white with the pressure. A few observers noticed that there was something in his hands but it only emerged later in the day that the item was a rosary beads.

But it was the student's appearance that caused the greatest stir. Gone was the lean, handsome young man who had appeared in Midleton District Court just ten months before. Back then, his hair was styled in popular fashion, with blond highlights. Now, Wayne O'Donoghue had visibly aged. His hair was now dark and plainly cut. He had put on substantial weight – his face was clearly heavier, almost swollen. Photographers and reporters who had attended his appearance in court on the previous 17 January were shocked at the transformation.

Then, with smooth precision, Wayne O'Donoghue was arraigned and the first drama of the trial emerged. When asked if he was Wayne O'Donoghue, the defendant stood and in a firm voice replied, 'Yes.' But when the court registrar then asked him how he pleaded to the charge of murder facing him, O'Donoghue said: 'Not guilty to murder, guilty to manslaughter.'

Prior to that statement, we had no inkling that Wayne O'Donoghue would enter any plea to manslaughter; in fact, most of the reporters attending the case had presumed it would be a straight-forward trial where the defendant would simply deny murder. We thought that any consideration of manslaughter would arise only towards the conclusion of the trial when the State's murder case could be better weighed against the defence position. Now, for the first time in public, Wayne O'Donoghue had admitted his involve-ment in the eleven-year-old's death.

As he silently resumed his seat and the bowed-head posture that would become his norm throughout the three-week trial, reporters for radio stations and evening newspapers raced to file copy. There was no longer any doubt over the identity of Robert's killer – the only issue now was intent.

*

After a short break to allow for the selection of the foreman, the jury of seven women and five men filed back into Court. Mr Justice Paul Carney, Ireland's most experienced judge of the criminal court, had already explained their duties to the jury and the running format of the case. Because of the defendant's arraignment statement, the trial was now about a single issue: whether Wayne O'Donoghue had intended to kill Robert Holohan. He had admitted manslaughter or the unintentional killing of the boy, but he vehemently denied his murder.

Before Wayne O'Donoghue's statement, he could have faced a number of outcomes: from 'guilty' or 'not guilty' to murder; a total exoneration; or, potentially, the jury could have been allowed to con-sider a 'guilty' or 'not guilty' verdict to the lesser charge of manslaughter.

To Mr Justice Carney's left sat the State team led by Shane Murphy SC, who was assisted by Sean Guerin BL and solicitors from the office of the Director of Public Prosecutions (DPP). To the judge's right sat the defence team, led by Blaise O'Carroll SC and Tim O'Leary SC. They were instructed by solicitor Frank Buttimer, who operated a large criminal law practice in Cork, just yards from the courthouse. From covering Cork Circuit Criminal Court matters over the previous decade, I was quite familiar with the defence team, which had to rank as one of the most experienced in the business.

In the public gallery to the rear of the courtroom, sat Wayne's parents, Ray and Therese. Both looked visibly shattered, Ray O'Donoghue's face white with stress.

THE STATE'S CASE

Shane Murphy SC, in opening with an outline of the State's case, said that O'Donoghue admitted to Det. Sgt Peter Kenny on 16 January: 'I am a murderer.' Mr Murphy said the detective, who was asked to call to the O'Donoghue home that day by the defendant's father, Ray, just twenty-four hours after Robert's burial, found Wayne in an armchair 'shaking and in a distressed state'. The State outlined that O'Donoghue said: 'I grabbed him by the neck. I did not mean it. It was an accident. I am a murderer. I am sorry. He [Robert] was like a brother to me.'

Murphy went through the events of that fateful day, step-by-step, quoting from Wayne O'Donoghue's statement to the Gardaí. The jury was told that the schoolboy had died from asphyxia, and the State claimed that this was as a result of a confrontation with Wayne O'Donoghue outside his home on 4 January. Mr Murphy said that, given the major difference in size and strength between the two, and O'Donoghue's actions subsequent to Robert's death, the offence represented murder. He also said the State would, through the trial, offer evidence from State Pathologist Dr Marie Cassidy that Robert might have suffered a blow to the mouth, and had his neck or throat compressed for between fifteen and thirty seconds as there were pin-point haemorrhages found on his skin behind his ears and inside his mouth. Marks on Robert's ribs also indicated that his chest had been compressed either by arms gripping him or by someone sitting astride him. Bruises to his back, shoulder and buttocks indicated he might also have been pushed up against a solid surface.

The State also outlined how, speaking to Det. Sgt Kenny on 16 January, O'Donoghue explained that a confrontation arose because he would not drive the eleven-year-old to McDonald's in Midleton for a milk-shake. After failing to persuade him to drive him to Midleton, O'Donoghue claimed to Gardaí that Robert began throwing stones at his car. 'Robert picked up gravel stones and threw them at the rear of the Fiat Punto car. I walked out to him. I put my right arm around his neck. I can't describe how tight I held him. It seemed very short. I released my grip and he just slumped down to my feet. I did not intend to cause him any injury.'

O'Donoghue had insisted to Gardaí that he was 'panicking'. He brought Robert's body into his home, laying it on the bathroom floor as he desperately splashed water on the boy's face to try and revive him. The State told how, after realising the boy was dead, Wayne O'Donoghue then dried Robert's face with tissue paper, wrapped the body in plastic bin bags and prepared to dispose of it.

'He dried the boy's face with toilet paper, and then flushed it away,' Mr Murphy explained. The State then said that O'Donoghue put the body in the boot of his car and drove it to the isolated area of Inch to dump, stopping only at a garage to buy a bottle of Lucozade. 'I just stopped the car. I got out and I opened the boot. I wanted to remove the body. I threw the body into the ditch,' O'Donoghue told the Gardaí. After dumping Robert's body in the isolated ravine, some twelve miles from Ballyedmond, Wayne O'Donoghue returned home where, at

5.50pm, he received a phone-call from a worried Majella Holohan asking whether or not he had seen her son with whom he was very friendly.

She was concerned about Robert because he was very afraid of the dark and he had not come home before darkness fell. O'Donoghue denied seeing Robert that afternoon, but then, several hours later, he returned to Inch with a container of petrol to set fire to the bin bags around Robert's body. However, statements that O'Donoghue subsequently made to Gardaí revealed that he found it difficult to locate the body in the darkness at Inch and he had to get on his hands and knees in the ravine before he could start the fire. The plastic bags only partially burned, though the State said its evidence would show that there was scorch damage to Robert's T-shirt and track-suit bottoms. The State also stated that forensic evidence found fingerprints from Wayne O'Donoghue on the plastic bags.

Mr Murphy also pointed out that, in three separate Garda interviews before the dramatic statements on 16 January, Wayne O'Donoghue had given no indication of what had happened to Robert Holohan or where his body might be. O'Donoghue had also taken part in the huge search operation for Robert on six different days. At no point did he attempt to direct searchers towards the area where the body lay or offer advice, even anonymously, on what had happened to the boy. The body was only found thanks to Garda technical experts and their use of technology linked to Robert's mobile phone. It took the huge search operation nine days to locate the body at Inch strand on 12 January.

The jury was told that the State would be presenting its case in segments, with evidence from key Garda forensic experts, State Pathologist Dr Marie Cassidy, as well as from Robert's parents, Majella and Mark, and other Midleton locals.

Shortly after 4.00pm, the State concluded its opening and called its first witnesses, Det. Garda Laura Bolger from the Garda Technical

Bureau and Det. Sgt Brian Goulding from Midleton, both of whom offered evidence regarding case photos. This was a standard precedure whereby every map and photo used, both by the State and the defence, during the case had to be verified and authenticated. Shortly before 4.30pm, the case was adjourned for the day and Wayne O'Donoghue, before being led out by prison officers, managed a short glance over at his parents.

*

As I walked out of the courthouse, I was beginning to wonder, as were many of my colleagues, about the strength of the State's case. It appeared to us that the prosecution were relying on circumstantial evidence to prove intent, largely focused on Wayne O'Donoghue's actions between 4 January and 16 January when he finally admitted his involvement in Robert's death to Gardaí.

Despite a frenzy of speculation before the case, there were no major forensic revelations. In the twenty-four hours before the trial opened I had learned that the material which had underpinned the change in charge from 'manslaughter' to 'murder' back in April would not now be introduced. That directive had apparently come straight from the DPP's office. So the State's murder contention now rested entirely on the case outline we had already heard. There were to be no evidential 'surprises'.

Likewise, there seemed to be little evidence regarding a motive. And while there were at least six more days of State evidence to come, I began to wonder whether the State would have enough hard evidence to cast doubt on Wayne O'Donoghue's version of what precisely happened at his house that day.

WEDNESDAY, 30 NOVEMBER 2005
THE TRIAL, DAY TWO

Most objections to media coverage occur on the second day of a criminal trial, and, judging by the pile of newspapers in front of the defence team, many of them marked and underlined, today would prove no different – causing a great deal of anxiety among reporters. Before evidence could even begin to be presented, the defence team formally objected to a number of media reports from the opening day of the trial. Blaise O'Carroll SC cited the *Irish Examiner*, the *Irish Sun* and the *Irish Mirror* over elements of their coverage. Central to their complaints were reports that Wayne O'Donoghue had attempted to set fire to the *body* of Robert Holohan. The defence team stressed that this was never stated nor claimed in evidence, but, rather, that the defendant had attempted to set fire to *plastic bags* around the body. The defence vehemently objected to any suggestion that the defendant had attempted to do more than burn the bags. One headline specifically brought to Mr Justice Carney's attention was: '*Strangled, Dumped and Burned*'. The defence also complained about broadcast reports on TV3 and Cork local radio station, 96FM.

Mr Justice Carney acknowledged the complaints but bluntly stressed to the defence that it was not his policy to abandon trials over media coverage if at all possible. But, in a further aside, he also commented on a radio report that I had just done for Cork's County Sound breakfast show with Patricia Messenger, saying that the arraignment and the jury selection had been mentioned in reverse order. It was now abundantly clear that every line of trial coverage would be scrutinised and extreme care would be required, not just for newspaper and TV reports but also for the daily round of live radio commentaries that now had the nation transfixed.

And, with that, the second day of evidence began, with brief submissions about maps of East Cork from Garda cartographer, Catherine

Walsh. These included maps of Ballyedmond and Inch, the two areas central to the search operation. It was the final piece of technical evidence required before the trial could move into testimony from the main witnesses.

*

The first major witness for the State was Robert's mother, Majella. Complete silence descended on the courtroom as the State called her to the witness box. The mother-of-three rose at 12.10pm to begin her evidence, pausing briefly as her husband, Mark, squeezed her hand in a silent show of support. Majella moved slowly but determinedly through the courtroom and across to the witness box to the right of Mr Justice Carney. After taking her oath in a strong but clearly emotional voice, Majella was then methodically taken through the events of that terrible day, 4 January, by Shane Murphy SC.

She explained that 4 January began as a very ordinary day. She was watching her children play, preparing their meals and greeting relatives who came to call. 'My father, William Murray, called with some scones around lunchtime [to Ballyedmond]. I think it was around 1.00pm. He didn't stay very long. I offered him lunch but he said he had to go home. He asked Robert did he want to go to the horses. But he [Robert] was riding out the day before so he decided to stay and play with the bike that he just got for Christmas,' she explained. After her father left, Majella said, she began her housework, with her two youngest children, Harry and Emma, playing indoors. Robert, who had been outside earlier in the morning, decided to go back out and play with his bike.

'Robert was in and out on his BMX bike. He went out the drive and swung to the right. I think he then went down the hill. He was wearing his black Midleton GAA track-suit bottoms, Nike runners, an orange top and his black Nike jacket. He was going fast but I thought at least he has his [warm] coat on,' she said. Majella calculated that the time was around 2.30pm.

Majella began to weep as she described her desperate efforts later that day to discover where Robert had gone. She told the Court she tried repeatedly to contact him from shortly after 3.30pm, but without success. She left a message on his mobile and kept trying to get through. Eventually, Majella described how she sent her daughter, Emma (8), to the neighbours' houses to see if Robert was there.

Amongst the first places the child checked for Robert was the O'Donoghue home where the eldest boy, Wayne, was regarded by Robert as more of an older brother than just a good friend. 'Robert adored Wayne,' Majella said. 'He looked up to him as if he was an older brother. We never had any problems with the O'Donoghue family,' she explained. When Robert failed to return home by 4.30pm and she couldn't get through on his mobile, Majella decided to ring Wayne.

Majella Holohan sobbed: 'He said he hadn't seen him [Robert] since 2.30pm that afternoon.' She added that she found Wayne O'Donoghue 'normal' that day. 'Later, Wayne called to our house and offered his assistance, along with his father and brothers,' she explained.

After Robert's BMX bike had been found, she told how she had asked Wayne to identify it for her. Majella added that Wayne told her: '"Don't worry, we will find him all right. I will try him on his mobile and he will answer my number."' The engineering student then tried to ring Robert on his mobile in front of Mrs Holohan. 'He put the phone up to his ear. But he said there was no answer,' she said. Robert had saved his money from Christmas to buy the Nokia mobile phone which he then shared with his mother, only buying the handset on 28 December, just seven days before his death.

As Robert's disappearance triggered a huge search operation, Majella recalled that Wayne was to the forefront of the search effort. Wayne supported the search for Robert on six different days, and called into the Holohan home three times to offer support. He even suggested areas to search for Robert to Mark Holohan. The Holohans were deeply grateful for all they thought the young man was trying to do for them.

'I offered him tea. He said, "Don't worry, we will find him." I thanked him. I told him he was too good and he was doing loads,' Majella Holohan sobbed. The Holohan family were so appreciative of all they thought that Wayne had done for them that, in the days after their son's body had been recovered, they even considered asking him to read one of the Prayers of the Faithful at his funeral Mass on 15 January, she explained.

The following day, 16 January, Wayne O'Donoghue made his first statement about killing Robert to Gardaí at his Ballyedmond home. Shane Murphy asked Majella Holohan about her reaction when she first heard the news. She told the hushed courtroom that she was 'astonished' when Gardaí informed her that Wayne had made a statement admitting his involvement in Robert's death.

*

As Shane Murphy finished for the State, Blaise O'Carroll SC began the defence cross-examination of Majella Holohan, focusing his questions on a syndrome Robert suffered from, Attention Deficit Hyperactive Disorder (ADHD). Mrs Holohan confirmed that her son was on Ritulin, a medication for the disorder which significantly eased the symptoms. He was prescribed the medication after going to see a specialist.

Robert had been finding it difficult to concentrate in school, and the Ritulin was found to ease significantly the symptoms of ADHD. However, once he was outside the classroom environment for any period of time, such as Christmas or summer holidays, his family allowed him to stop the medication while he pursued his outdoor interests.

Majella confirmed to Mr O'Carroll that, for the duration of the Christmas holidays, Robert was not taking the medication. 'He had a very mild form of ADHD. He was only taking one tablet a day. But he was off his medication on the holidays. He didn't believe in Santa but he was very excited about the whole Christmas. The whole atmosphere was wonderful. We were all in very good humour,' Majella explained.

Asked to describe her son, Majella revealed that her son was almost a mirror image of herself. 'I would say he was probably a replica of myself. He was a bit of a dreamer. He loved life. He thought everything was beautiful and that everyone was wonderful. He was a typical eleven-year-old. Robert was a normal, happy, beautiful child,' she stated.

Mr O'Carroll also questioned Majella about the contacts between Wayne O'Donoghue and her son and the fact that Wayne had been extremely generous with his time to Robert. Majella said that she thought there was nothing unusual about the friendship between her son and Wayne O'Donoghue. She told the Court that Wayne had once built a tree-house for Robert in the back garden, and that, when he got his Fiat Punto car he would regularly take Robert and another young-ster from the area, Heather Harte (13), for spins. Sometimes he would take them both to McDonald's for an ice-cream or a milk-shake. On other occasions he would take them for a DVD.

Mr O'Carroll summarised: 'Wayne was, to all intents and purposes, a generous person to Robert and Heather.'

*

Majella, by now composed, resumed her seat in the courtroom as her husband, Mark, took the stand, likewise to be taken through the events of that terrible day by the prosecution. He arrived home from work, he told the Court, at 5.30pm on 4 January to find his home in turmoil. He explained to the Court that when Majella said Robert was missing, he immediately became concerned. 'I was worried because it was getting late and he [Robert] was afraid of the dark. Normally, he would be at home before it got dark.'

By 6.30pm, Mark said the entire family were getting 'panicky'. Mark tried ringing his son's mobile but got no response. 'I rang Robert's phone a few times, but to no avail. I said: "Robert would you get in contact with us. We are trying to find you. Will you ring home",' he said. As word of Robert's disappearance spread, he said, neighbours began to gather to offer help. Mark and Majella searched Midleton town centre and all the estates where they thought Robert might have gone, but with no success.

When they arrived back to Ballyedmond, Mark told how he had met Wayne and his brother, Timmy, who offered to help with the search for Robert. Wayne said they would search a forest where Robert used to play. The Gardaí later arrived and the search began in earnest. Mark described the next nine days of searching for Robert as 'a total nightmare'. 'We were praying that he would turn up alive,' he said.

Tragically, those hopes were dashed on 12 January when search volunteers found Robert's body at Inch, and Mark Holohan said that the family were shattered by the discovery. Just four days later they were even more shocked when Supt Liam Hayes personally called to their home to explain that their neighbour, Wayne O'Donoghue, had admitted involvement in Robert's death. 'I just couldn't believe it,' the father-of-three said. 'Wayne would have been in my house from time to time. I didn't see him as I would be at work,' he said. Mark added that his son idolised his older neighbour: 'Robert looked up to Wayne – he idolised him.' Mark also said that his son would be taken by Wayne to McDonald's, Fat Al's snooker club and even to Xtra-vision for DVDs.

Questioned about the type of child Robert was, Mark stressed that he was energetic, fun-loving and devoted to outdoor pursuits, particularly horses and horse-riding. 'He was a very lively child – he really loved sports. Robert was also fairly good with his hands. Physically, he was a fairly strong lad.'

Cross-examined by Blaise O'Carroll, Mark Holohan acknowledged that, at times, Robert could be difficult and demanding. In particular, he would often press his father to play hurling or football with him when he returned from a long day at his construction business. 'I'd often blame myself for being tired and not going out to play with him,' Mark said.

Mr O'Carroll also queried whether Robert had thrown temper tantrums and how Mr Holohan had coped with them. 'He would, no doubt about that,' Mark Holohan replied. 'I used to slap him and say you are to stop. Sometimes he might be defiant. I often blame myself for slapping him because of my own tiredness.' He said that if he did slap Robert, it was across the back of the legs.

*

Next to give evidence was Robert's grandfather, William Murray, who, when he took the stand, explained how on 4 January he had called to his daughter's Ballyedmond home. He had offered to take Robert to see the horses but, tragically, the little boy decided to stay in Ballyedmond to play.

Mr Murray emphasised to the Court how Robert had idolised Wayne O'Donoghue. Wayne was 'like a God' to Robert, he said. 'He [Robert] loved him,' Mr Murray added. He also said that Robert was a very loving grandson, and was absolutely devoted to animals, particularly horses.

*

After members of Robert's immediate family concluded their evidence, the State called testimony about how the boy's bike was found. Tom Keohane Snr and Thomas Keohane Jnr both confirmed how they had spotted the silver bike placed in the ditch downhill from the Holohan home at Ballyedmond on the evening of 4 January. Neither knew who owned the bike but, because of the lateness of the evening and the way the bike was placed in the ditch, they decided to bring it home for safe-keeping until the owner could be found.

Local man Michael Daly then told the Court he had spotted Robert Holohan playing near the gate of his home shortly before lunch that day as he drove by, while three other witnesses, Helen Murphy, Gerard Crowley and Catherine White, confirmed that they saw a bike in the ditch shortly after 5.00pm that evening. Critically, a number of witnesses – Phyllis Smith, Sharon Smith, Simon Forrest, Katie Forrest, Patrick McDonnell, Mark Keohane and Paul Cashman – testified that they had not seen the same bike as they passed along the same route at various times around 3.00pm.

The second day of the trial hearing ultimately heard from a total of twenty-six witnesses called by the State, the majority offering testimony about 4 January and what they saw in Ballyedmond that day. None had seen anything out of the ordinary or even remotely suspicious. But their evidence began to provide a rough timeframe for when Robert was last seen and when his bike could have been placed in the ditch at Ballyedmond.

As the evidence concluded, I left the courtroom, clear that Majella Holohan's evidence was the dominant aspect of the day. I knew her emotional testimony regarding Robert's last day and the desperate search for him would be the main news item of the day. In fact, her heartbreaking revelations about what she went through that day dominated both radio and televisions news bulletins for the entire evening. A trial which had always threatened to grip the imagination of the nation was now dominating press, radio and TV bulletins. Reports on the case were even being carried in Northern Ireland and the UK. Everyone seemed transfixed by the question: What exactly had happened to Robert Holohan on 4 January?

THURSDAY, 1 DECEMBER 2005
THE TRIAL, DAY THREE

The first inkling of suspicious behaviour on the part of Wayne O'Donoghue in relation to Robert's disappearance was related by Gardaí on the third day of the trial – as well as the first flash of emotion from Wayne O'Donoghue.

Inspector Martin Dorney, one of the Midleton Gardaí who led the hunt for Robert, took the stand for the State and explained how, on 9 January, the sixth day of the search operation, he had a bizarre confrontation with Wayne O'Donoghue and his brother, Timmy. He told the jury how the weather that day was absolutely appalling and, because of the high winds and heavy rains, it was decided to restrict the search operation because of safety concerns for the volunteers, particularly in areas of difficult terrain. 'I was approached by two young men [Wayne and Timmy]. Both behaved in an aggressive manner to me. I explained to them what was happening. Basically, what was said to me was that there was sufficient light left in the day and the search should continue elsewhere,' he said. Inspector Dorney said that he also noticed during the search operation that Wayne O'Donoghue seemed extremely interested in the maps in the co-ordination centre which depicted the areas being searched by volunteers.

That version of events was corroborated by another Garda, Det. Sgt Brian Goulding, who testified that he was confronted by Wayne O'Donoghue during the search operation and warned that daylight was being lost while the search teams were being briefed by the Gardaí and then deployed to assigned areas.

'He was not happy with my reply,' Det. Sgt Goulding explained. He added that, like Inspector Dorney, he noticed how interested the student seemed to be in the search areas. 'He would come and see what areas had been searched and what areas we had pencilled in to be searched,' he said.

Once again, the defendant maintained a bowed-head posture throughout the proceedings. The only time there was any glimpse of emotion came when some of his school and college friends testified, when called by the State, about the events of 4 January. John Hutch, Robin O'Shea and Paul Foley had all known Wayne for over a decade. Paul had been friends with Wayne since fifth class while John, who, like Wayne was a third-level student in Cork, was amongst a group of teens that socialised together. Now, all three would be questioned about their contact with the defendant on 4 January and on the subsequent days while the search for Robert was ongoing.

As Hutch began to describe how he first heard about Robert's disappearance while he was in Cork, Wayne O'Donoghue abandoned his bowed-head posture and gazed intently at his friend.

Hutch said he was in Cork preparing for college when Wayne rang him to say that Robert was missing. He met Wayne the next day after Wayne had returned from searching for the boy. Paul Foley told the Court that, over the coming days, Wayne told him he had been questioned by the Gardaí about Robert's disappearance. 'He just seemed normal,' Paul recalled. He later met Wayne on the day of Robert's funeral. 'I didn't know what to say. I thought he had lost a friend. He was just down and very sad-looking,' he said. Robin O'Shea, who was also studying in Cork, told the Court that he had gone out on 4 January to watch an English soccer match when Wayne called him on his mobile. 'He said that Robert, his neighbour, was missing,' he said. After Robert's body was found at Inch, O'Shea recalled that Wayne seemed 'shaken and upset'.

Later, State witnesses told the Court how Robert was apparently searching for friends on the afternoon of 4 January. Liam Tully, who has two daughters, one older and one younger than Robert, heard a knock on his Ballyedmond door that lunchtime. 'Robert was there with his bike at the door and he asked where the girls were,' Mr Tully said. He explained that they had gone out with their ponies and Robert thanked him and left. Mr Tully didn't see the eleven-year-old again. Two other witnesses, Roisin Bell and Mary Daly, told the Court how they had seen Robert on his bike that day, and Robert had waved to Mary Daly as she passed by in her car.

If the Garda witnesses had raised suspicions about Wayne O'Donoghue's behaviour during the nine-day search operation, other volunteers now offered evidence which added to those concerns. Bizarrely, while out searching for Robert with volunteers, O'Donoghue was actually challenged by one man about whether he had killed the eleven-year-old. Andrew O'Callaghan told the Court that, after hearing that O'Donoghue was the last person to see Robert and then being told by the twenty-year-old that he had had a row with the boy that day, he decided to challenge him. 'I turned around and I said: "Did you kill him?" He didn't open his mouth once after that,' the witness said. He said O'Donoghue was talking with a group of search volunteers and the subject was whether Robert had been abducted or killed. It was only later that Mr O'Callaghan said he realised precisely whom he had been speaking to.

A number of witnesses also said they felt uncomfortable with Wayne O'Donoghue, his behaviour and his interest in what areas were being searched. Bertie Madden told the Court that O'Donoghue explained during the search operation that he had refused to take Robert to the chipper the day he disappeared. Mary O'Brien testified that O'Donoghue said to her during the search that Robert had been in his house that day, and when, on 12 January, they overheard a Garda saying on the radio that a body had been found she suddenly felt O'Donoghue was very withdrawn. 'He just went quiet. He didn't say anything. It seemed like a very awkward silence. I don't know how long it went on,' she said.

Another search volunteer, Tim Leahy, who was assisting the search effort in the Guileen area near where Robert's body was ultimately found, said he met O'Donoghue, whom he didn't know at the time, and felt 'very uncomfortable' in his presence. He noted that a gold-coloured hatchback, similar to that owned by the defendant, was parked in the area for some time that day.

The courtroom was hushed as two witnesses, Tom Deely and Martin Sloan, each explained how they had discovered Robert's body on 12 January while searching undergrowth near Inch strand. The two friends had searched in the Whitegate area earlier that day but had moved on to Inch where they were focusing on deep undergrowth along a steep ditch which ran parallel to the access path to the beach. 'I had a stick and Martin had a hurley,' Tom Deely said. 'It was mostly briars and grass along the ditch as I was walking along. I was rooting away in the briars. Then, in the ditch, I noticed a leg. There was no shoe on the foot. I saw a bit of a black track-suit on the legs. I could only see the legs of the body. Then the Gardaí were called.'

*

When Det. Sgt Peter Kenny of the elite National Bureau of Criminal Investigation (NBCI) took the stand at lunchtime, the case took another dramatic turn. Det. Sgt Kenny read through a number of statements that Wayne O'Donoghue had made prior to and including the dramatic admission on 16 January of how he had killed the eleven-year-old.

Det. Sgt Kenny had been on duty in Midleton at lunchtime on 16 January with Det. Garda Michael O'Sullivan when they received a phone call from Wayne's father, Ray. He asked them to come to his home at Ballyedmond as a matter of urgency. 'He informed me that his son had related to him that he had killed Robert,' the detective said. The two Gardaí immediately went to Ballyedmond where they found Wayne O'Donoghue in the sitting room of his home, shaking and in a distressed state.

The detective garda took the Court through his notes, taken after caution, of what Wayne O'Donoghue said as he admitted that he had killed Robert: 'I did it – I am a murderer. I am sorry. He [Robert] was like a brother to me. If I could switch roles with him I would.' The Court learned that, earlier that day, O'Donoghue had gone to buy the Sunday newspapers which were dominated by the coverage of Robert's funeral from the previous day as well as the appeal by the Bishop of Cloyne, Dr John Magee, for the killer to hand themselves in.

Kenny continued: 'O'Donoghue told me he bought the *Star* but said that: "I didn't read it all because I was too upset." After briefly chatting with his girlfriend, Rebecca, he told me that he finally decided to tell his father, Ray, about his involvement in Robert's death. "I was upset. I said [to myself] this is not right. I said I was going to go home to tell my Dad. I went up to him and said I love you and I am sorry. It was an accident. He said, 'What do you mean?' I said it was an accident what happened with Robert."' He [Wayne] told how [a stunned] Ray O'Donoghue, after realising what his son had just said, began crying and immediately called his wife, Therese, and they went out to the garden shed to clarify what their son was saying, partly so their other two sons would not overhear and become upset.

Det Sgt Kenny stated that Wayne O'Donoghue told him that he was crying, as was his father, Ray, when he had finished relating the precise circumstances of Robert's death. Kenny continued: 'Ray O'Donoghue decided he immediately had to notify the Gardaí and, because of the distressed state Wayne was in, his mother, Therese, stayed with him in the garden shed amid fears he might try to harm himself.'

Kenny then said he cautioned Wayne and, following legal advice given to Wayne by the family solicitor, proceeded, with Det. Garda Michael O'Sullivan, to take a seven-hour statement from the student. Ray O'Donoghue initially contacted the family's solicitor, Dan Wall, but Wall had advised, in the light of the seriousness of the matter, that a specialist criminal law solicitor should be contacted. He recommended Frank Buttimer. Mr Buttimer immediately agreed to travel to

Ballyedmond and he was present as Gardaí commenced to take the written statement from Wayne O'Donoghue. Over the duration of that afternoon, Wayne refused several offers to stop and take a break, continuing for a total of seven hours until the statement was concluded shortly before 9.00pm. The only request O'Donoghue made before the Gardaí formally arrested him was to be allowed a visit from his girlfriend, Rebecca.

O'Donoghue insisted to the detectives that the confrontation which led to Robert's death was a total accident and that he had not intended to harm the eleven-year-old. In his evidence, Det. Sgt Kenny said Wayne insisted he had only grabbed Robert by the throat after he claimed the boy had thrown pebbles at his head and Fiat car outside his home. 'I am deeply sorry for what happened,' he told the Gardaí. 'Robert was a good friend and almost like a brother to me. If I could switch roles I would. What happened was a fluke, an accident.'

Initially, after realising that Robert was dead, O'Donoghue told the Gardaí he was traumatised, shocked and that he planned to kill himself. 'I looked in the [bathroom] mirror with a kitchen knife in my hand and put the knife to my throat.' But, panicking, the twenty-year-old said he opted to get rid of the body before his mother returned home, deciding that after dumping the remains he would later hang himself with wire from a tree in the back garden. However, after returning from dumping Robert's body, O'Donoghue claimed he became caught up in the frantic local search effort for the schoolboy.

'I just went with everything,' he told Gardaí. As time wore on and the twenty-year-old took part in the search effort on six different days, he admitted to Gardaí that he found it increasingly difficult to reveal what had happened to Robert. 'As each day went by, I felt the hole getting bigger. Each day it seemed harder and harder,' he told Det. Sgt Kenny.

But what he had done to Robert continually nagged at him. 'I was thinking how disrespectful it was where I had put the body and what I had done to a friend. To place the body in the middle of nowhere where it wouldn't be found. I said to myself that I had to go back and remove the body from where I had left it and place it on the beach and get rid of the plastic bags so the body would be found.

'I had also decided when I had carried out this I was going to come home and, when everyone was gone to bed, I was going to hang myself from the tree in the corner of the garden. I was going to remove the bags and burn them; I was telling myself this was the way it had to be.'

Garda Kenny told the court how Wayne said that his effort to remove the body from the ditch at Inch failed. 'I started talking to the body, saying "Rob", as if he were alive.' But, in the end, he told the detectives he was forced to leave the body where it was and abandon his plan to place it on Inch beach.

The jury also heard details of the previous statements O'Donoghue had made to Gardaí before his admission on 16 January. In one statement, taken one week before his admission of involvement in Robert's death, Wayne claimed he had heard 'screams' from the Holohan house and told Gardaí that Majella found it very difficult to control Robert. In this statement, O'Donoghue also claimed that he had heard Robert calling his mother 'a bitch' and 'a slut'.

In another statement, made on 8 January to Det. Sgt Kenny, O'Donoghue insisted that he had not seen Robert Holohan since refusing to drive him to McDonald's. He told Gardaí: 'There was a knock on the door. Robert Holohan was at the door [on January 4]. He asked me would I bring him to McDonald's for a chocolate milk-shake. I have done this a number of times. It was a perfectly normal request. I said no, and gave the reason that the traffic was heavy. He [Robert] said, "Don't be an asshole" and I said, "F… off." I was pissed off with the girlfriend over her [Leaving Cert] study timetable.' At this point, O'Donoghue claimed that the eleven-year-old had cycled away and that he did not see him again.

*

As the third day of the trial concluded, those of us covering the case were increasingly aware that it now appeared the prosecution would rely very heavily on the evidence of State Pathologist Dr Marie Cassidy for an explanation of precisely how Robert died and an outline of the events surrounding his death. So far, the State had offered a graphic account of the events before and after Robert died, such as what he did in the hours before he died and the search operation for him after 4 January. But there was little evidence on those crucial few hours on the afternoon when the little boy died.

With the defence yet to call any witnesses, the consensus among the media, and a few Gardaí watching proceedings, was that nothing in the trial had so far substantially contradicted Wayne O'Donoghue's contention that Robert's death was a tragic accident.

CHAPTER 7: THE TRIAL, days 4-6

FRIDAY, 2 DECEMBER 2005
THE TRIAL, DAY FOUR

As the trial concluded its first week, the State now began to call several key witnesses, not least of whom would be Wayne O'Donoghue's girlfriend, Rebecca Dennehy. It was also clear that the prosecution case would take at least another full week to conclude, though, in one concession, Mr Justice Carney was told that Mr Murphy SC and Mr O'Carroll SC had agreed on several witness statements which could be read to the trial rather than having the witnesses called in person to offer evidence. Ultimately, more than fifty witnesses would be dealt with in this fashion, significantly shortening proceedings.

The petite, attractive girl stood up in the body of the court and walked slowly towards the witness box. Rebecca Dennehy didn't pause to look at Wayne O'Donoghue as she took the stand but every eye in the room flicked from one to the other. Wayne, once again in his head-bowed posture, briefly gazed up as his blond girlfriend swore to tell the truth and nothing but the truth to the Court.

In hushed, nervous tones the nineteen-year-old began to explain to State prosecutor, Sean Guerin BL, how she had first begun dating Wayne in May 2004 and how she was shocked by his involvement in Robert Holohan's death.

Rebecca painstakingly went through the events of 4 January, casting a remarkable light on what Wayne O'Donoghue had done on the day Robert died. Mr Guerin asked what contact Rebecca had with Wayne on 4 January. She explained that she lived just a few minutes away from Wayne's house and had been talking to him on the phone at 1.00pm that day. A short time later he arrived at her house. 'Wayne had been lecturing me about studying,' she explained. 'He came to help me with a study timetable for my Christmas revision [exams].' Wayne left her house to go on an errand for his brother. 'His brother Timmy rang him to say that he had bought an exercise bike in Cork. He wanted Wayne to collect the bike [in his car].' Rebecca then spent some time with a friend before deciding to ring Wayne so they could complete work on the study timetable and her college application form.

Mr Guerin asked when she next had contact with her boyfriend. 'He [Wayne] sent me a text,' she said. 'It was after 4.00pm but I cannot remember exactly. He said he was doing college stuff and his mother had put a virus disk into the computer and he was checking it. He sounded normal. He just said he would come back later,' she added. But what Rebecca didn't know was that, by this time, Robert Holohan was already dead.

Later that evening Wayne returned to the Dennehy home and together he and Rebecca watched 'The Simpsons' on TV. Mr Guerin asked whether there was anything strange or unusual about her boyfriend: 'He seemed fine. I can't recall [the conversation] – it was probably chit-chat,' Rebecca said. Later, Wayne had to go home and Rebecca decided to accompany him. 'It was Wayne's turn to walk the dog, so we took him up the road. We strolled up the road and back again.' After returning, they played a PlayStation computer game for about twenty minutes in Wayne's room before he remembered, around 7.00pm, that he had to drop a DVD back to Xtra-vision. They went to Xtra-vision together and dropped the movie into the express return box before Wayne drove Rebecca to her home. The couple parted and Wayne said he had to do some work. 'He said he was going to sort out some college stuff,' she said.

Mr Guerin then asked her about the last time she had met with her boyfriend that night: Rebecca confirmed that Wayne returned to the house a third time that evening. '[It was] about 8.30pm ... I was watching "The Swan" on TV3 at the time,' she added. Mr Guerin asked whether there was any mention of Robert Holohan. She said that for the first time Wayne told her that his friend, Robert, was missing.

Later, after leaving the house, he contacted her on her mobile phone. 'He seemed normal. He said they were just looking for Robert. He said a few people were in the [Ballyedmond] woods. They were all out searching for Robert. He said he [Robert] had called earlier and asked him to take him to McDonald's but Wayne said traffic was too bad. He said: "I feel like it's my fault. If I had taken him to McDonald's maybe he would still be around." He seemed very upset and worried,' she said.

But Ms Dennehy insisted to Mr Guerin that her boyfriend was not crying at the time and that she first noticed he was upset after he had been questioned by the Gardaí in the next few days. Because he was the last person to see Robert, he felt that Gardaí thought he might be involved.

Mr Guerin then questioned Rebecca at length about how her boyfriend seemed over the coming days when the search for Robert Holohan was at its height. Rebecca admitted that she thought Wayne was increasingly worried about his neighbour and good friend. 'There were times when he was very quiet. There were times when he was very agitated. He would say he was fine, but I knew different,' she said.

Mr Guerin asked her what changes she noticed in him. On occasions, she said, O'Donoghue was unusually quiet and withdrawn, which she put down to worry and concern for Robert. He also told her the Gardaí had been 'a bit hard' on him during the first interview he gave but, she said, he felt the second interview was 'a bit easier'. O'Donoghue made a total of four statements to Gardaí before 16 January, one of which took the form of a written questionnaire – the questionnaire was handed out on 5 January to everyone in the the the general Ballyedmond area. O'Donogue's other statements were made on 5 and 8 January, both at Midleton Garda station. The final statement was taken on 9 January at his home by Det. Garda Michael O'Sullivan to clarify issues that arose in the statement taken the previous day.

'He did say once or twice that because he was the last to see him [Robert], that they [Gardaí] might think he was involved,' she said. However, in the days after Robert's body was discovered, O'Donoghue also told his girlfriend that he thought the Gardaí were close to making an arrest.

When asked by Mr Guerin about what Wayne thought of his dealings with the Gardaí, she replied: 'I think he was upset by the whole thing. He said there was a profile of what they thought the abductor looked like. He said it looked like they [the Gardaí] were close to making an arrest. He said that they [the Gardaí] probably thought he was involved.'

*

In cross-examination by defence counsel, Blaise O'Carroll SC, Rebecca Dennehy spoke of her relationship with Wayne and what she noticed about her boyfriend that January. She had met Wayne in May 2004 and immediately fallen in love with him. 'I would see him more after school and especially at weekends,' she said.

Asked by O'Carroll had she ever met Robert Holohan with Wayne, she said that once she started going out with Wayne she met the youngster. 'I was walking up from town [in summer 2004] and Wayne was parked at the Spar garage and he had Robert and Heather [Harte] in the car. He was bringing them to town for an ice-cream. Robert was hyperactive, a typical eleven-year-old.'

Mr O'Carroll asked her how she thought Robert and Wayne had seemed to 'gel together'. She replied: 'I always thought they got on well together. Wayne was mad about Robert and Wayne treated him like a younger brother.' Rebecca stressed that, during her time with Wayne, she had never seen him get angry or annoyed with Robert. 'It was always typical boys' [stuff] – they liked the PlayStation and stuff. They just got on really well.' She stressed that she had never heard Wayne make any kind of derogatory remark about Robert.

Mr O'Carroll asked whether, in her contacts with Wayne over the coming days, she noticed any changes in his demeanour. Rebecca, who also took part in the search for Robert on three different days, admitted that she had noticed changes in her boyfriend. 'There were times when he was extremely quiet and usually Wayne would be talking non-stop, but there would be times when he was into himself. There were times when he would call and be gone again, and he was up and down and agitated. During that morning – the morning of 16 January – when he left he did not kiss me, which is unusual.'

Mr O'Carroll asked whether she had noticed changes in her boyfriend in the days after January 4. 'I thought Wayne was upset. One evening I was on the phone once or twice and knew by the way he sounded that he was very down. He just kept very quiet and said he was fine, but I knew differently. He said he was fine, but I knew he was upset.'

Mr O'Carroll asked what was Wayne's demeanour when she was asked to call to his Ballyedmond home on the evening of 16 January so he could tell her in person what had happened to Robert. 'He looked wrecked. He was tired and he was crying and shaking. It was horrible,' she said. Rebecca acknowledged that she was shocked by the whole experience.

Mr O'Carroll queried whether she had ever gone to Inch with her boyfriend. She said that, after Robert's body was found in the ditch at Inch, Wayne brought her to the scene in his car. 'We drove down and I stayed in the car and Wayne got out, put some flowers down and said a prayer and we drove back.'

Mr O'Carroll said that Rebecca had described her contact with Wayne before 4 January as 'a touchy-feely kind of relationship'. She said that they had always kissed when saying goodbye. Rebecca explained that she was surprised when, on 16 January, O'Donoghue left her home earlier that day without kissing her goodbye.

The nineteen-year-old broke down and wept as she described her feelings for Wayne to defence counsel, Blaise O'Carroll SC. She said she had known the defendant since she was twelve or thirteen years old and found him a wonderful boyfriend. 'I just cannot comprehend how it happened,' she said. 'Wayne is just such a good person. It broke my heart to hear it.' Rebecca also said that Wayne got on very well with her parents and they greeted him 'with open arms' in their home.

Rebecca related how she loved the defendant – and, despite all that had happened still felt the same way about him. 'I love Wayne to bits – and I still feel the same way about him,' she sobbed. 'I just cannot comprehend what happened. Wayne is just such a good person. It broke my heart to hear it. Wayne always treated me like a queen from the day I first met him. He was always there for me when I needed him, day or night. He is brilliant. I just get on really, really well with him. He is genuine and caring. I couldn't fault him personally. I love Wayne to this day and I really feel the same way about him.' After composing herself, she left the witness box and resumed a seat in the public gallery that she would maintain for the remaining six days of the trial.

*

But if Rebecca Dennehy's evidence was emotional, its impact was matched by the first display of a trial exhibit, with Majella Holohan breaking down and sobbing as Gardaí produced the clothes that Robert was wearing the day he died and described in terrible detail the scene where his body was recovered.

Garda technical expert Det. Sgt Thomas Carey, told the jury that the terrain at Inch where Robert's body was discovered was so difficult that officers had to use a mechanical 'cherry-picker' to access the site without disturbing evidence. There were brambles and undergrowth covering the steep incline and Gardaí also had to use special scaffolding ladders. 'It was a very, very remote area,' he said.

There was absolute silence in the packed courtroom as Det. Sgt Carey turned to an evidence officer and, donning special rubber gloves, opened the clear plastic bags to produce the T-shirt, track-suit bottoms and underpants Robert was wearing when his body was discovered on 12 January. The boy's T-shirt, trousers and underpants showed clear signs of scorch or burn marks. The T-shirt was burned by its tail while the waist-lines of both the underpants and the track-suit bottoms were scorched.

Det. Sgt Carey said that, when he was examining the scene at Inch, he noticed 'a dense, tar-like coating on the uppermost level of briars'. Robert's body was lying head down in the thicket and, such was the incline, his legs were almost vertical to the sky. He explained to the Court that, from the level of the pathway, it was almost forty feet to the base of the ravine. Robert's body was covered by two black plastic bin-bags and looking through tears in the plastic it was clear that animals had already inflicted damage on the body.

Robert's Nokia 3200 mobile phone, which was not operational, was still in the boy's right-hand trouser pocket. As the scene was processed by Garda forensic experts, Robert's two Nike runners were found, one of which was in the black refuse sack while another runner had a plastic bag shoved up into its toe. A white Killeen refuse sack was also found with what appeared to have been a blood stain on it. Several hair fibres were noted and taken for analysis. Det. Sgt Carey explained that an examination of the clothing revealed mud stains on Robert's track-suit bottoms while Gardaí also noted that, beneath the body, a number of twigs appeared to have been scorched. Det. Sgt Carey said a close examination showed similar traces of the tar-like substance that was found on the upper briars.

Later, Det. Sgt Carey said he had conducted detailed analysis of Wayne O'Donoghue's Fiat Punto car, his Ballyedmond home and the garden shed behind the house. He also analysed the stones on the O'Donoghue's gravel driveway. O'Carroll's junior, Tim O'Leary SC, held up a glass jar containing gravel-type stones and asked if they were the same type as those Carey had examined. Carey said they were, and O'Leary confirmed that those stones had been taken from the O'Donoghue driveway; however, there were no further questions about the matter.

In further technical evidence, Garda fingerprint expert Patrick O'Brien confirmed to the Court that an examination of two plastic bags found inside the refuse sacks by Robert's body, revealed two finger-print samples. Starting from 13 January, twenty-four hours after Rob-ert's body was discovered, the samples were painstakingly removed and stored. These were then analysed and compared with some elimi-nation samples already taken as part of the Garda investigation. On 15 January, the samples were found to match the right index finger and second left middle finger of Wayne O'Donoghue.

TUESDAY, 6 DECEMBER 2005
THE TRIAL, DAY FIVE

The new-look Cork courthouse had only opened its doors the previous summer and now the high-tech, flat-screen TV monitors that lined the walls of courtroom No. 2 would be used in a trial for the first time.

Such was the historic nature of the event that Mr Justice Carney allowed photographers in to film the facilities before the trial resumed. The screens would not only be used to play Wayne O'Donoghue's three video-taped interviews with Gardaí but would, for the first time outside Dublin, allow a witness to give real-time evidence via video-link in a murder trial.

The jury were to view the tapes of three interviews given by the defendant in Midleton Garda station on 17 January, twenty-four hours after his first statement of admission of responsibility for Robert's death to detectives. The first tape consisted of the entire transcript of O'Donoghue's statement being read back to him by Det. Sgt Peter Kenny and Det. Garda Michael O'Sullivan.

Under modern criminal procedures, a written statement can be taken from a defendant, and this is then, in major cases, put to the individual during a video-taped session. The benefits of this are that it allows the jury to judge for themselves the demeanour of the accused, how the Gardaí handled the interview session and in what context answers are offered to certain questions. Once the video-tape of the original statement is taken it often occurs that further, follow-up questions are also put to the accused.

In this case, in the first video tape, Det. Garda Kenny read through the statement which Wayne O'Donoghue made on 16 January to verify its accuracy. It amounted to little more than reading a full transcript of the seven-hour written statement taken the evening before.

The second video tape consisted of a question-and-answer session conducted a short time later with Wayne O'Donoghue by Det. Garda Sean O'Brien and Det. Sgt Brian Goulding. This was also conducted at Midleton Garda station, but differed dramatically in both mood and tone. The questions pursued by the Gardaí were intended to clarify various issues arising from the first video-taped interview and to raise several issues not fully dealt with in the first session.

The third and briefest tape dealt with O'Donoghue being asked to identify a number of evidential items, ranging from Robert's bike to a petrol can taken from his family home. Of the three, the second tape was undoubtedly the most fascinating as the two Gardaí probed, in robust detail, the admission statement O'Donoghue had made just hours before.

THE FIRST VIDEO TAPE

A packed courtroom watched avidly as the first video tape relayed across three giant screens a visibly nervous Wayne O'Donoghue listening as Detective Garda Peter Kenny read out a statement of how Robert had died. O'Donoghue appeared in the video wearing a casual top, slacks and a baseball cap. His agitation was evident from how he shifted in his seat and repeatedly stretched his neck as the Garda officer began the painstaking reading of his detailed seven-hour admission statement from the previous evening. Det. Garda Kenny started reading the written statement in front of O'Donoghue, which began by explaining how the twenty-year-old had decided the previous day to tell his father how Robert had died.

On tape, Det. Sgt Kenny carefully read O'Donoghue's statement about the events after the Gardaí first arrived at his home on 16 January and his explanation of how Robert died. When Gardaí arrived at the O'Donoghue home, Wayne was in the sitting room, sitting in an armchair and in a very distressed state. Det. Garda Kenny read from the transcript, quoting Wayne: "'I am a murderer and I am sorry. Robert was throwing stones at the car and I grabbed him by the neck. It was an accident. I didn't mean it. It was an accident. He was like a brother to me.'"

Det. Garda Kenny read out Wayne's explanation of how, on the day he finally confessed to Gardaí, he had got up early. "'I got up at 10.00am today [16 January], got dressed and went down to the Spar shop and was looking at the papers. I bought the *Star*. I was reading bits and pieces but I could not read it all because I was getting too upset. I went to see my girlfriend, Rebecca. It was about 11.15am. I went in and we chatted for about two to three minutes. I left after about five minutes. I was upset and I knew it was not right so I decided to go and tell my dad.'"

In the statement, Wayne then explained that he went back to

Ballyedmond and steeled himself to tell his parents what had happened to Robert. Det. Garda Kenny read: "'I went into his room and he was in bed alone and it was dark. I started crying and I said, 'I love you', and 'I'm sorry. It was an accident and I didn't mean it.' He asked me what I meant. I told him it was an accident what had happened with Robert. I said, 'He was throwing stones at my car and my head. I asked him to go and gave him a nudge and pulled him away from his bike and the bike fell to the ground. I grabbed him by the throat by my left hand and said: 'Will you stop with the fucking stones.'"'

The transcript revealed that when Wayne told his father, Ray, he was deeply shocked and became distressed. Det. Garda Kenny read out that, after realising the enormity of what his son had just said, Ray O'Donoghue immediately alerted his wife, Therese, who was away from the house. When she returned, the trio went out to the garden shed so as not to disturb their other two sons. When Therese heard Wayne's story she begged him to tell her it hadn't happened. Det. Garda Kenny read out that Wayne had explained: "'Mum said, 'Please tell me it isn't true, please tell me it isn't true.' We were crying and hugging. I told them it was an accident and I loved Robert and that he was like a brother to me. I knew him for five to six years. He was a good friend.'"

The taped transcript then focused on the precise sequence of events that Wayne O'Donoghue claimed led to Robert's death on 4 January. It revealed how Robert had first called to the O'Donoghue home shortly before lunch while Wayne was in the garden playing with the family dog. Robert joined in and they played football for a brief period. Wayne then went back into the house and Robert left. Wayne briefly went into Midleton to meet his girlfriend, Rebecca, before returning to Ballyedmond.

Det. Garda Kenny read Wayne's words: "'I went to collect my bag and returned home at 2.30pm. There was no one in. More or less straight away, about 2.35pm, there was a knock and when I opened the door Robert Holohan was outside. Robert wanted me to take him to McDonald's for a chocolate milk-shake. I had just been into town a number of times and said No, as the traffic was very heavy. Robert called me an asshole and I told him to 'Fuck off' and he went away. This would be normal between us and no offence was intended or taken.'"

The tape continued with Wayne explaining to detectives that, less than an hour later, just as he was preparing to start a written college project on the morals of abortion, Robert returned. Det. Garda Kenny read: '"He came in and he was in the kitchen searching for a can of Coke. This was not uncommon. He asked me to bring him to McDonald's and I said No, as I still had lots to do. Robert went past me to the front door and I followed him.

'"Robert went towards his bike and as he was picking it up he was popping pebbles at the car and I said to him: 'Robert, will you grow up.' He then threw a bunch of pebbles at the rear end of my car. I walked over to him to give him a nudge and told him to 'Fuck off.' I then turned and felt more pebbles hit the back of my head and my car. I was not over-happy with him. I walked over to him and put my right arm around his neck and jerked him away from the bike towards the car. I released the grip with my right hand and was still holding him with my left hand at the scruff of his neck. Nothing was said between us.

'"I moved my left hand up to his Adam's apple and I said: 'Will you stop with the fucking stones?' I cannot say how tight or for how long I held him but I did not intend to cause any harm or injury. When I released my left hand from his throat he just fell to the ground. I didn't realise he had been hurt. He slumped to my feet and I called his name a few times. I thought it was a joke. When I could get no response I realised something was wrong.'"

On the video-tape, Wayne O'Donoghue took a sip of water, and then continued to listen as Det. Garda Kenny continued with the transcript explanation of how, in growing panic, the twenty-year-old decided to bring Robert's prone body into the house to try and revive him. He carried the boy in through the front door and decided to lay him down on the bathroom floor.

Det. Garda Kenny read: "'I lay him down and called his name a couple of times again. I had no knowledge of resuscitation techniques and if I had I would have used it. I lifted up his arm and it fell straight down. I said, 'Oh, my God.' I think I believed at that stage that he may have died. I came into the kitchen wondering what I was going to do next. I don't know how long I was in the kitchen. This was about 3.50pm. I was thinking, 'What I will do?' I was really panicking. My mother and brother were due home shortly. I went back into the bathroom, hoping he would stand up. I listened for breathing or for a response, but there was none.'"

Det. Garda Kenny read out that, for the first time, Wayne O'Donoghue considered suicide as his only realistic option: "'I went into the kitchen to the right-hand side drawer and took out a knife. I was in complete shock about what I had done or what had happened. I cannot describe my feelings, but my intention was to cut my throat. I had the knife in my right hand. I went into the bathroom and looked into the mirror while I held the knife close to my throat. I took away the knife and put it down by my side and then went back to the kitchen and threw it back into the drawer.'"

The transcript explained, in Wayne's own words, how he proceeded to change his mind and opted to dispose of the body first before the O'Donoghue family returned home to Ballyedmond. He planned to commit suicide later that night. Kenny read: "'I was panicking and thought about removing the body. I knew about having black bags in my room. I got them from a pub where I used to work [The Goose's Acre in Midleton]. The black bags were in the bottom of the wardrobe. This was all done in panic. I went into the bathroom with two bags.'"

Wayne said that, having returned to the bathroom and realised, with mounting horror, that Robert was dead, he got the body ready for placing in the black plastic bags. He explained that he washed Robert's face with some toilet tissue which he then flushed down the toilet. But O'Donoghue said to the detectives that he couldn't explain why he did this.

Garda Kenny read: "'I then pulled one bag over his head and the other on his legs. I can't recall whether they covered his body completely. I carried the body out to the car and I closed the boot and put his bike on the back seat. I went back into the house and I was still in a panic. I was thinking: 'What will I do with the body?' I was trying to get everything cleared up before Mum came home. I rang Rebecca and told her I would be down in a while. I left home at 4.10pm. I got into my Punto and I started it up and reversed round the side of the house. I turned left up the hill and turned around again and came back down the road.'"

In the statement Wayne explained how, stopping a short distance down the road, he decided to get rid of the BMX bike. "'I got out of the driver's side and took the bike and put it in the ditch. I think the bike was facing towards the golf-driving range.'"

The transcript revealed how Wayne looked around but saw no-one. He then drove off, still desperately trying to decide what to do with the body of the boy now wrapped in black plastic bin bags in the car boot. Garda Kenny read Wayne's words: "'I pulled into Foley's garage. I just parked the car. I was in the car wondering what I would do now. I got out and went into the shop. I was upset and crying. I had a look around and bought a bottle of Lucozade and returned to the car. I got back into the car and drove back towards home. I had no idea where I was going or what I intended to do. I kept driving on and on. It was getting dark and my mother would be home and I was still panicking. I knew I had to go somewhere.'"

O'Donoghue said that, at one point, he was shocked to see a Garda car behind him on the road. "'A Garda squad car was behind and I was panicking more. I thought it might be pulling me over for speeding and I knew if he pulled me in he would know there was something wrong.'" But the Garda car drove off in another direction and Wayne then found himself driving towards the coast.

Garda Kenny read: "'I went up Whitegate Road and I went up the hill and took the next left and drove along until I saw the beach. I knew I could not leave his body on the beach. My early intention was to place him on the beach so he could be found.'" Wayne's statement explained that he saw a silver car parked along by Inch strand and knew that he could not leave the body on the beach here. But his desperation was mounting and he simply wanted to get Robert's body out of his car. "'I just wanted to remove the body. I pulled the boot up, walked to the right and threw the body into a ditch. Before I did it I threw his trainer into the ditch. I threw both into the same area and the plastic bags were still on the body. I did all this very quickly. I was in a state of panic. I was crying and I was very upset. I got back into the car and drove home. It was around 5.00pm.'"

Det. Sgt Kenny read how Wayne said he then decided to call to see Rebecca first – and knew that he had to act as if nothing had happened. "'I knew I had to act normal. I drove to her house at 6.00pm and 'The Simpsons' were on the TV. I went to the sitting room where Rebecca was. I had no clue what was going on.'"

But, while trying to outwardly act normally, he said his thoughts were in turmoil over what had happened, and particularly how he had treated the body of the boy who regarded him as an older brother. "'It was disrespectful where I had placed the body. It was in the middle of nowhere and it would not be found. But I knew I had to maintain the appearance of a normal routine. I returned to my house and walked my dog. It was now 6.45pm and after a short walk I returned to the house and played on the PlayStation.'"

Wayne's script explained how, slightly earlier, he had already received a phone call from a worried Majella Holohan and he admitted that he had denied seeing Robert that afternoon, insisting he hadn't seen him since lunchtime. After leaving Rebecca, Wayne decided to revisit the scene at Inch to try and place the body on the beach as he insisted he had originally intended. "'I went to my room and decided what I would do, which was remove the body, place it on the beach and get rid of the plastic bags. I also decided when I carried out this I was going to hang myself from a tree in the corner of the garden when everyone had gone to bed.'

But he said, via the transcript, that he had also brought a plastic bottle filled with petrol from a container in the family garage. The tape revealed that this was to burn the plastic bags and nothing more. He explained that the combination of panic, the darkness and the nature of the terrain at Inch made it very difficult for him to find where he had placed the body. Garda Kenny read: "'I looked for about twenty to twenty-five minutes before I found him. And I then started talking to the body as if he were alive. All I could see was the black bag so I grabbed the bag but I could not get the bag out as it was caught in briars. I was not wearing gloves and could not see the body, and I poured some petrol on the black bag and set the bag alight. The bag was partially lit. It was only lit for a while and then I put the torch back on and I could see a leg. I knew from the position of the body I would not be able to get it out so I walked back and looked for an entrance."'

But, after three quarters of an hour of scrambling through briars and nettles, O'Donoghue said he finally realised that he could not retrieve the body. Wayne said he eventually decided to return home and was immediately confronted in Ballyedmond with an escalating search operation for Robert. "'I went searching with everyone for him until around 5.00am. I then went back [home] at 7.30am."'

On the tape, he explained that, as time wore on, it became increasingly difficult to maintain a normal façade. Garda Kenny read: "'It was more difficult to carry out my plan. Every day it seemed harder and harder and I didn't tell anyone what happened until I told my father. Two days ago I shook out the [car] mats because I was carrying around people but I did not clean out the boot.'"

Det. Sgt Kenny reached the end of the statement and Wayne O'Donoghue's expression of regret. "'I am deeply sorry for what happened. Robert was a good friend and was like a brother to me. If I could swap roles then I would. I did not intend to harm him. What happened was a fluke. It was an accident. I am sorry I did not come forward earlier to explain what happened.'"

As the tape finished we realised it had merely elaborated on the statement from Wayne O'Donoghue that Det. Sgt Kenny had already read onto the record. But it was fascinating to watch Wayne O'Donoghue in the courtroom watching Wayne O'Donoghue on the video tape listening to his first detailed statement of admission of involvement in Robert's death. The tape showed a young man who was visibly nervous and clearly under enormous pressure. But what struck me was the slight nervous convulsing of the neck and jaw muscles that Wayne seemed to engage in throughout. Not to mention the almost alarming contrast between the lean young man on the screen with the blond highlights in his hair and the heavier, almost bloated individual in the dock.

THE SECOND VIDEO TAPE

The second video tape was substantially different in tone and mood to the first. This tape consisted of an interview in which Det. Garda O'Brien and Det. Sgt Goulding examined, in precise and often robust detail, O'Donoghue's crucial statements. The opening of the interview underlined just how radically different the two tapes would prove to be when O'Donoghue was immediately challenged about his earlier statements. Det. Garda O'Brien asked O'Donoghue whether all his earlier statements to Gardaí were 'horseshite'. But O'Donoghue insisted on tape that his seven-hour statement of 16 January was accurate.

When questioned by the two detectives about the nature of his relationship with Robert, he insisted that it was perfectly normal. 'It probably would be [unusual] if you were living in an area like where you have your own age groups, but we are living in the country. The way I have always seen it, like, you have different age groups, from my age at the eldest right down to as young as Robert's younger sister. Often she would play with us sometimes as well, like. We were very good friends, I would say.'

Det. Garda O'Brien pointed out that he had had a car for almost a year, allowing him the freedom to socialise with people his own age. But Wayne insisted to the Gardaí that the freedom to travel out of Ballyedmond only came with his car, and that had only been a recent acquisition. 'I have only the car for approximately ten months now so I had good relationships built up with my neighbours, and Robert, a good five years before I even got the car. That relationship was sustained always, even when I had the car. The car was kind of like a novelty to the – this might sound stupid – a novelty to our area because I was one of the oldest there and I was obviously the first to get a car. I would take them [the younger children] for spins and down to McDonald's and stuff, like, as I would do for Robert, as I would do for Heather [Harte] as I would do for any of my other neighbours.'

The two detectives focused specifically on the events that led to Robert's death. Det. Garda Goulding asked what Wayne was doing when Robert called. O'Donoghue insisted he was working on his studies. 'I was in my room. I was looking over my speech on abortion. It was roughly 3.15pm and the door bell rang. I opened the door and it was Robert Holohan.'

The detectives asked about the college speech that O'Donoghue was working on, to be told it was about abortion and that Wayne O'Donoghue was arguing from the position that it was wrong and a crime. He said he needed to have the project finished and ready for his return to Cork Institute of Technology (CIT) after the Christmas break.

O'Donoghue then said Robert walked into the kitchen and began rooting around. 'He walked freely in and went in the kitchen like he would normally do if my parents weren't there. He started rooting through the fridge and cupboards nearby.' But Wayne said he asked Robert to leave: 'Jesus, Robert, would you ever go away. I'm trying to get this [college] speech done.' He was leaving and, on the way out, he was saying again, like: 'Will you bring me to McDonald's?' Robert had asked that before, Wayne explained, 'and I had said "No". I then followed him out, like. I don't know was he pissed off because I wouldn't bring him down town or whatever, but he started popping stones at the car. It was not vigorous, but like flicking them [the stones] at the car.'

Wayne said he told the boy to go away and admitted Robert was now beginning to annoy him. After what he insisted was 'a nudge' to get Robert to leave, he felt the pebbles being thrown at his back. 'Then I turned around – I kind of got him – the best term is a headlock. I dragged him away from his bike. He was not going flying or anything. But I did drag him away from the bike and the bike did fall. I was a bit annoyed at this stage. To be honest I wasn't calm. I was annoyed then I grabbed him with my left hand around his neck.'

Det. Garda O'Brien queried, on the tape, precisely how O'Donoghue had caught the eleven-year-old and O'Donoghue got out of his chair and demonstrated to the two detectives the nature of the grip he placed on the boy. But O'Donoghue repeatedly insisted to the two detectives that he never intended to hurt or injure Robert. 'There was never any intent. It was probably a bit vicious but there was no intent when I was doing that. There was never any intent.'

But Det. Garda O'Brien queried what O'Donoghue meant by 'intent'. Wayne replied: 'Obviously to do what happened, like, you know, obviously, he is dead, like. There was no intent to harm him. I don't know. Like, Christ, like.' But the detective persisted, querying what O'Donoghue intended to do by placing the young boy first in a headlock and then grabbing him by the throat. He asked: 'Are you seriously saying there was no intention to harm him [Robert] after you put him in a headlock, swung him around and then put him up against the car and grabbed him around the throat?'

But Wayne O'Donoghue was adamant he did not intend to hurt Robert. 'There was no intent. There was no malicious or vicious intent there at all. There was no malicious intent. There was no intent there, you know. It is hard to describe it.'

O'Donoghue – who had declined offers to have a drink or take a break from the interview – when queried by the detectives, stressed that he had not lost control. 'No. No, I did not flip the lid. I was not calm – as I already said, I was annoyed. But there is a difference – I was not calm, but I did not flip the lid. I was annoyed and never once in my head did any intent come in to harm the boy. I was annoyed. I did not flip the lid. I was not calm. I was annoyed. We have clarified that already. I was annoyed.'

Det. Garda O'Brien asked how long O'Donoghue had kept the boy in the headlock. O'Donoghue stressed to the detectives that he cannot recall. 'Well, I can't remember the period. I did not time what I was doing. I just cannot remember how long. I had held him firmly, you could say. You might say this is kind of stupid now, but I cannot really remember the length I was there. I was just: fucking stop throwing the stones, you know. Like, just fucking stop. But at the time I did not think that I was squeezing too hard. I was just there: will you just fucking stop with those stones. I just said fucking stop. I do not remember how many times I said it.'

Once again, O'Donoghue insisted to the detectives that he was shocked when Robert collapsed at his feet when he released his grip. 'I removed my hand and he just sort of slipped. Kind of slouched down. He did not fall on the gravel or anything like that. He just slouched down around my knees. At first there was no immediate panic.' O'Donoghue said he shook Robert gently by the shoulder but got no response. He said he then repeatedly called, 'Rob, Rob', but to no avail.

'I panicked. I knew when he was not calling back to me that there was something wrong. So then I carried him into the bathroom – I suppose so no one would see it when driving past. I thought maybe that if I brought him in and threw some water over him – I just did not know it was serious at that time. It's hard to describe, but I was panicking. I was in a state of panic.'

O'Donoghue said he got no response when he threw water on Robert in a bid to revive him – and his panic grew. 'He was lifeless. When I lifted up his arm it went straight down. I was completely and utterly panicked. I cannot describe the feeling I had. Unless you are in that situation you cannot describe the feeling.'

Det. Garda Goulding asked why O'Donoghue did not simply contact the emergency services? O'Donoghue explained, on tape, that he tried to listen for any sounds of breathing, but, because he was not trained in first aid, he did not know what to do to revive the boy. 'People looking at it from the outside are [saying]: "You should have rung the police, an ambulance or even your parents." But it is hard to describe what it was like. To be honest it [a 999 call] did not even come into my mind at all. [Nothing] like: Jesus I had better ring the ambulance. It was total shock. Total panic.'

O'Donoghue repeated his claim that he contemplated suicide, but decided against it having taken a knife from the kitchen. 'I don't know why I didn't do it. I was probably a coward. I do not know why I couldn't do it. Basically, I would say I was a coward. I don't know what came over me. I have a family that love me. I have a girlfriend who I really love. I was probably just a coward. But I was going to cut my throat.' Det. Garda O'Brien simply commented: 'But you didn't.'

O'Donoghue explained to the two detectives that he did not know what to do next. 'I stayed there looking at Rob for a while. It could have been a minute or two. I was just in a daze. I was just staring. I just cannot describe what I was thinking. I was in a total daze. I didn't know what to do. I was going around the place in total shock and panic. [Then] I was going around the kitchen – I suppose with my head in the air. I just did not know what I was doing. It was all panic. Everything was done in a panic after that.'

Mr Justice Carney halted the video evidence at this point with the interview to be resumed the next day.

WEDNESDAY, 7 DECEMBER 2005
THE TRIAL, DAY SIX
THE SECOND VIDEO TAPE CONTINUED

Once again, the sight of Wayne O'Donoghue in the dock staring at Wayne O'Donoghue on a plasma TV screen describing how an eleven-year-old boy died was nothing less than surreal. The defendant blessed himself before the day's evidence began and once again rosary beads were visible in his hands. By now, the massive national coverage the case was attracting had ensured that the public gallery was filled on a daily basis.

The video-taped interview resumed with O'Donoghue vehemently denying that he had ever attempted to stop Robert screaming or crying out for help.

'Did you at any stage put your hand over Robert's mouth to stop him screaming?' Det. Garda O'Brien asked. 'No, never at any stage did I do that,' O'Donoghue insisted. When challenged if he was sure, the defendant replied: '110 percent.' O'Donoghue was also adamant in the interview that he had never attempted to burn Robert's body and that he had not wanted to place the remains on the beach so that they could be washed out to sea.

Det. Garda O'Brien questioned O'Donoghue about his actions after slouched down around my knees. At first there was no immediate panic.' O'Donoghue said he shook Robert gently by the shoulder but got no response. He said he then repeatedly called, 'Rob, Rob', but to no avail.

'I panicked. I knew when he was not calling back to me that there was something wrong. So then I carried him into the bathroom – I suppose so no one would see it when driving past. I thought maybe that if I brought him in and threw some water over him – I just did not know it was serious at that time. It's hard to describe, but I was panicking. I was in a state of panic.'

O'Donoghue said he got no response when he threw water on Robert in a bid to revive him – and his panic grew. 'He was lifeless. When I lifted up his arm it went straight down. I was completely and utterly panicked. I cannot describe the feeling I had. Unless you are in that situation you cannot describe the feeling.'

Det. Garda Goulding asked why O'Donoghue did not simply contact the emergency services? O'Donoghue explained, on tape, that he tried to listen for any sounds of breathing, but, because he was not trained in first aid, he did not know what to do to revive the boy. 'People looking at it from the outside are [saying]: "You should have rung the police, an ambulance or even your parents." But it is hard to describe what it was like. To be honest it [a 999 call] did not even come into my mind at all. [Nothing] like: Jesus I had better ring the ambulance. It wa' total shock. Total panic.'

O'Donoghue repeated his claim that he contemplated suicide, b' decided against it having taken a knife from the kitchen. 'I don't kr' why I didn't do it. I was probably a coward. I do not know w' couldn't do it. Basically, I would say I was a coward. I don't]' what came over me. I have a family that love me. I have a girl' who I really love. I was probably just a coward. But I was goin; my throat.' Det. Garda O'Brien simply commented: 'But you d'

O'Donoghue explained to the two detectives that he did r'

realising Robert was dead. O'Donoghue maintained to the two detectives that he was in a state of panic that day and had no initial plan of what to do. 'I did not have a clue where I was going [with the body]. I did not have an idea. Jesus Christ, I hadn't a clue, like.' The twenty-year-old insisted he had only set fire to the black plastic bags in which he had wrapped Robert's body and then dumped into a steep ditch so he could see precisely where the remains were. 'It was so that I could see,' he insisted. The detectives queried why he had set fire to the bags. O'Donoghue said that, when he returned to Inch where he had dumped Robert's remains, he found it difficult to see in the undergrowth and to pull the black plastic bags out of the ditch. 'I tried to get the black plastic bag back. I was getting a grip on it but it was caught on briars and everything.'

Despite having a torch, O'Donoghue said the black plastic bag was reducing his visibility and making it impossible to recover the boy's remains so he could place them on the beach. At this point, he poured petrol onto the bag and set fire to it with a lighter he said he kept in his car. Det. Garda O'Brien asked where that lighter was and O'Donoghue replied that he had thrown it in the bin at his home. When questioned by the detectives, O'Donoghue admitted that he does not smoke. He insisted he was still panicking – and it never entered his head to tell his parents, the Gardaí, a doctor or a priest what had happened. 'I was totally and utterly stricken with panic. I was all over the place. I was really ashamed of myself,' he said.

The detectives again asked why he just didn't tell someone what had happened? O'Donoghue explained that he didn't tell anyone what had happened because of the pressure he was under. 'All my friends, my family, my neighbours – everything just got on top of me.'

When further challenged by the detectives about how Robert died, O'Donoghue again insisted that the confrontation and its tragic outcome was not intentional. '[It happened] Accidentally – and with no intent,' he stressed.

Det. Garda O'Brien asked why he had returned to Inch strand. O'Donoghue insisted that his purpose in revisiting the scene at Inch was to try and put Robert's remains on the beach where they could be found. 'I thought it was disrespectful what I had done,' he said. But the incline and the position of the body made that impossible. And he insisted [again] that his purpose in setting fire to the plastic bags with the petrol was to try and see whether the body had slipped down the steep incline. 'All I could see was the black bag. I couldn't see anything else. I assumed that Robert's body had slipped down [the incline]', he said.

The second video-taped interview then concluded and the trial heard that the third tape, which involved evidential matters being placed before O'Donoghue, would be played on Friday. The trial also heard that while the State Pathologist, Dr Marie Cassidy, could begin her evidence, she would have to conduct her cross-examination via video-link from Dublin due to work commitments. This would take place the next afternoon.

*

A number of witnesses then offered evidence to the trial on the circumstances surrounding the nine-day search for Robert, the role Wayne O'Donoghue played in that search as well as Robert Holohan's ADHD condition.

State witness Sylvia Fielding, a friend of Majella's, explained that she met Wayne O'Donoghue during the search and felt that he was 'jittery'. She remembered at the time that Wayne was apparently the last person to see Robert.

Two volunteers, Aine Dorgan and Mick McCarthy, from the Irish Rescue Dogs Service told the trial how interested Wayne O'Donoghue was in their animals and whether the dogs could follow the scent of a person if that person had travelled in a car. Aine Dorgan said that she had joined the search operation for Robert on 5 January, and had her trained collie dogs searching the area around Ballyedmond. She met Wayne O'Donoghue and he immediately began asking her about her dog's tracking abilities.

'He asked if Robert was in a car would the dog pick up a scent? Then he asked what would happen if Robert was in a river? There were other questions along that line,' she said. She also recalled how Wayne O'Donoghue had said he was the last person to see Robert and how the boy had been off his medication for ADHD.

Aine Dorgan's colleague, Mick McCarthy, had also joined the search and was assigned a local guide – Wayne O'Donoghue. Mr McCarthy said he recalled O'Donoghue telling him about Robert and how he had a theory that the boy had gone to show off his bike. O'Donoghue described Robert as highly-strung and said that it was possible the boy had fallen into the river. He said that O'Donoghue had also shown interest in the possible use of bloodhounds – the best tracking dogs in the world – in the search for Robert.

The next State witness, Consultant Prof. Michael Fitzgerald, offered evidence on Robert's ADHD condition and how he had diagnosed and then treated it. He confirmed that he had assessed Robert for ADHD on two occasions, in October 2002 and again in April 2003. He explained that Robert was dyslexic and, given his general symptoms such as hyperactivity and inability to concentrate, he was satisfied the boy had both ADHD and another disorder, Oppositional Defined Disorder (ODD).

Prof. Fitzgerald described Robert's condition as 'moderately severe' and requiring medication. He added that the Principal of Robert's school, Midleton CBS, had also written to him asking him to support an application for extra resources for the boy. But, with regular treatment with the drug, Ritulin, there was great success in addressing the symptoms of the disorder.

Prof. Fitzgerald said that, after taking Ritulin, Robert showed a very positive response. But, the Professor acknowledged under cross-

examination by defence counsel Blaise O'Carroll SC, that once the
medication is stopped, the patient would relatively quickly revert to
their former status.

*

The Court then adjourned for lunch and, after it resumed, Mr Justice
Carney was informed that the next State witness was the State Pathologist, Prof. Marie Cassidy. (In the outline to the trial she was referred to
as 'Dr' Cassidy, but during her appearance in court she was called 'Professor' by both the State and the defence teams.) However, given the
length and complexity of her expected evidence, the defence team
would not have sufficient time in the remaining afternoon session to
conclude their cross-examination. So it emerged that Prof. Cassidy
would offer her State evidence today and would then, in a first for a
Cork trial, undergo cross-examination by the defence via video-link
from Dublin on Thursday afternoon.

Prof. Marie Cassidy took the stand amid a hush of anticipation. Everyone in Courtroom No. 2, from the Gardaí to the reporters, knew that
her evidence would prove absolutely crucial. The State's trial opening
had laid enormous emphasis on the disparity in size and strength
between Wayne O'Donoghue and Robert Holohan, so the pathology
findings of Prof. Cassidy were central to the prosecution's argument
that, such was the disparity in size between the two, the use of such
force on Robert could only have had one outcome. On the other hand,
everyone knew that the absence of such clear-cut indications would
only strengthen the defence's position that the boy's death was a tragic
accident.

Taking the stand, Prof. Cassidy confirmed that she was notified on
the afternoon of 12 January 2005 about the discovery of the body of
Robert Holohan and asked to travel to East Cork. She explained that
she arrived at the scene at Inch strand early on 13 January and conducted a painstaking preliminary examination. 'The body had been

found on a steep bank,' she told Shane Murphy SC. 'The head was pointed down. He was curled over into the foetal position.'

In the body of the Court, Majella Holohan began audibly to sob as the terrible scene at Inch was described in detail. Her husband, Mark, sat grim-faced as he listened to the condition in which his young son's body was found.

Prof. Cassidy said the boy was fully clothed but there was evidence that wildlife had been attacking the remains. 'There was evidence of animal damage to the legs, loins and also the head.' The upper portion of the head was badly damaged, she explained, particularly over the eyes; horrifically, it emerged that such was the level of animal damage that Robert's face was virtually gone from above his eyes. Both of Robert's legs, which had been pointing towards the sky and the upper path leading to the strand, had been particularly badly damaged by animals. The right leg was exposed to the shin bone, the tendons and the muscles. On the left leg, below the shin, all that was left was a strip of skin over the calf.

When Prof. Cassidy concluded her analysis at the scene, the boy's body was removed to the mortuary at Cork University Hospital (CUH) for a detailed post-mortem examination. It was believed that the cold weather had helped to preserve the scene and prevent insect activity. To further preserve evidence, the body was kept clothed and carefully removed to the hospital. 'The body was taken as it had been found,' she said.

While there was little doubt that the body was that of the missing eleven-year-old, dental records were used to confirmed that this was indeed Robert Holohan. Prof. Cassidy also confirmed that the clothing evidence shown earlier to the Court by Det. Garda Carey were the same items removed from the body: an orange T-shirt, black track-suit bottoms and dark blue boxer shorts underpants. She confirmed that, due to a fire, the material in the hem of one garment had actually melted.

The body was partially encased in a black plastic refuse bag. 'But the plastic was damaged and torn due to animal activity, exposing the top of the head,' Prof. Cassidy said. Robert died 'within hours of his last meal' and orange segments were found in his stomach.

Significantly she stated that there was no evidence of sexual assault. Likewise, there were no traces of alcohol or drugs found in the boy's system.

Prof. Cassidy explained that, in general, deaths from neck compression or manual strangulation can be very complex. A number of different factors can impact on the time period before death occurs. She said that violent struggles could have increased the boy's oxygen needs and therefore accelerated his death. But Prof. Cassidy said that while bruises to Robert's legs could have been caused by kicking out in a confined space, they are also relatively commonplace on active young boys.

Prof. Cassidy explained that she felt a key finding were pin-prick 'petechial' haemorrhages located behind Robert's ears, on his scalp and on the inside of his mouth. 'They were almost like a small rash,' she explained. These haemorrhages are caused, she said, by the compression of the neck and require such pressure to be exerted for between fifteen and thirty seconds. While a number of these 'petechial' haemorrhages were found, she said that other areas where they can also be found, such as around the eyes, could not be examined due to animal damage.

Questioned by the prosecution about that 15-30 second timeframe, Prof. Cassidy said it was 'an arbitrary figure.' It had been outlined in various medical textbooks but could vary depending on circumstances such as circulation etc. In general, she said it was accepted that 15-30 seconds of neck pressure were required to cause petechial haemorrhages.

A detailed examination of the body also found marks to Robert's ribs, indicating that he may have been restricted by having an arm tightly held around his torso or by having someone sit astride him. She said she also found imprints and marks from a necklace Robert was wearing on his neck, as if it had been forced into his skin, possibly during a head-lock or other such forcible hold.

Bruising to the neck muscles was 'subtle' and, she said, the pattern of injuries to the neck was consistent with manual strangulation. However, she said the force used on Robert was insufficient to damage or fracture his larynx. But the pathologist explained that it was extremely difficult to fracture the larynx of a young person such was the flexibility of the structure in that age group. As a person ages, the larynx becomes more rigid and, therefore, slightly easier to fracture. There was no evidence that a ligature was used in Robert's death.

'The post-mortem examination showed no evidence of significant trauma to this young boy,' she said. 'His death was due to asphyxia due to neck compression.' But a further examination of Robert's mouth revealed that he may also have received either a slap or had a hand held firmly over his mouth. The eleven-year-old's brain was swollen when examined and this was a clear indicator of hypoxia or acute oxygen starvation. The post mortem also revealed deep bruises to his shoulder, back and buttocks, indicating that he may have been held against a solid surface.

Vomit was found in Robert's throat but Prof. Cassidy said tests showed this was not a factor in his death, and more than likely occurred as the boy was dying. 'It was most likely an agonal event,' she said. While burn or scorch marks were found on Robert's T-shirt, track-suit bottoms and underpants, there was no burn damage to the body itself. Robert's skin was pale except in places where it had been bruised or discoloured due to the way he was lying.

Questioned by Shane Murphy SC about how long the compression could have been maintained on Robert's neck, she explained that it was very difficult to say for certain. The pathologist said that a number of different factors could impact on time-to-death. It was impossible for her to say precisely how long the grip had been maintained on Robert's neck to cause death.

The State concluded its examination of Prof. Cassidy and, given the time, Mr Justice Carney adjourned the trial until the following day. Prof. Cassidy would begin her cross-examination by the defence via video-link then.

CHAPTER 8: THE TRIAL, day 7

THURSDAY, 8 DECEMBER 2005
THE TRIAL, DAY SEVEN

Very quickly into the murder trial, the consensus amongst observers was that, having heard an outline of what Wayne O'Donoghue told Gardaí, the pathology evidence was going to prove crucial.

The State Pathologist, Dr Marie Cassidy, took the stand initially on Wednesday afternoon but underwent cross-examination by defence counsel, Blaise O'Carroll SC, on Thursday via special video-link from the National Detective Headquarters on Harcourt Street in Dublin. And what immediately emerged was that Dr Cassidy's evidence would be set against the opinions of Northern Ireland's State Pathologist, Prof. Jack Crane, who had studied both her post-mortem report and the pathology photos, though Dr Crane would not appear in court until the following day. The cross-examination revolved around Blaise O'Carroll putting Prof. Crane's main findings from his written report to Dr Cassidy. There was general agreement among those attending the court that how she dealt with these findings would be crucial to the outcome of the case.

O'Carroll initially reviewed the evidence given by Prof. Cassidy the previous day, and she repeated all the salient points. Then, in cross-examination, O'Carroll focused his attention on what Prof. Cassidy had *not* found and on the precise interpretation of what she *did* discover. He queried whether, in fact, her findings largely bore out what Wayne O'Donoghue had told the Gardaí had happened to Robert.

She agreed that her findings did generally corroborate Wayne O'Donoghue's account, but she rejected the suggestion made in cross-examination that injuries to Robert's mouth and ribs were 'minor' or 'trivial'. 'They cannot simply be thrown aside,' she said.

The defence put it to Prof. Cassidy that, in Prof. Crane's opinion, she had absolutely no basis for drawing conclusions from injuries to Robert's mouth and ribs. 'I don't agree with Prof. Crane,' she replied. 'I do hundreds of post-mortems every year and bruises in the mouth are not there unless there is a cause for them.' Such injuries had to have a cause, she asserted: 'There had to be trauma to this child's mouth. The mouth had been injured,' and she pointed out that while the precise cause could not be known it could have been caused either by a slap or by someone holding a hand firmly over Robert's mouth. 'They [the bruises] are an indication of trauma and they cannot just be thrown aside,' she declared.

Mr O'Carroll also said that Prof. Crane felt the indications that the child was in an arm-lock were very significant and that 'there was no sign of a violent struggle and no indication of extreme force being applied to his neck or throat.' But Prof. Cassidy insisted that there wereclear indications that the boy had had his neck compressed, with bruise damage to three layers of soft muscles in his neck.

The most critical point raised by the defence had to do with the vagal nerve. The defence team put it to Prof. Cassidy that accidental damage to the vagal nerve in Robert's neck (as a result of the headlock) could have been crucial in his death, and could have resulted in the boy dying even if the grip on his neck had been released after a very short time. She said that compression or interference with the vagal nerve can be a factor in such deaths, but she pointed out there were significant indicators that Robert's death was by neck compression-related asphyxia. 'But it's difficult to say how long that pressure was applied. All I can say is that the pressure on the neck was for sufficient time to cause the bursting of these blood vessels,' she stated.

The key difference here is that Prof. Crane maintained that the primary cause of death was the headlock and its effect on the vagal nerve, whereas Prof. Cassidy, though allowing for the headlock and the activity of the vagal nerve to be a factor, suggested that strangulation was the decisive act.

Prof. Cassidy stressed that the mechanism of death by asphyxia is 'very complicated' with the period-to-death being influenced by a significant number of factors. She largely agreed with Prof. Crane, who pointed out that: 'As regards death by asphyxia due to neck compression, there is really very little scientific evidence on how much force is necessary to effect it and for how long this force needs to be applied.'

Referring to her remark about pressure for fifteen to thirty seconds being required for petechial haemorrhages, Prof. Cassidy agreed that this figure was arbitrary but was drawn from textbooks dealing with asphyxia. 'Once the neck is pressed there are a lot of things that start to happen,' she said. 'There are a lot of things that can be started in motion and can continue even after the pressure is released.' But Dr Cassidy said it does require a specific amount of force to close a person's windpipe – a structure which is designed to avoid that very occurrence. She concluded her responses to the cross-examination by repeating that her findings were that Robert Holohan died from asphyxia due to neck compression.

*

As the coroner concluded, prosecutor Shane Murphy SC, began to call the last of the State's witnesses and the third video-taped interview with Wayne O'Donoghue at Midleton Garda station on 17 January was played. It detailed a list of items belonging to Robert Holohan, ranging from his 'Go Easy' BMX bike to his blue-and-white Nike runners.

Garda Colm Noonan also went through a list of the calls that Wayne O'Donoghue had made on 4 January, mostly from his own mobile. He explained that Wayne had had a mobile for about a year, and, like Robert Holohan's new mobile, it was a picture phone. O'Donoghue explained that Robert had taken a snap of a poster on his [Wayne's] bedroom wall. This depicted a joke road-sign depicting a match-stick student crawling across a road with a pint in hand. The slogan was 'Student Crossing'. O'Donoghue explained that Robert had taken this shot with his [Robert's] new mobile after he had purchased the phone.

The trial also heard Det. Garda John O'Shaughnessy list images captured of Wayne O'Donoghue from CCTV cameras around Midleton on 4 January. These showed him at various shops and petrol stations with his Fiat Punto, all about the time that he said he was *en route* to dump Robert's body at Inch. The final image, believed to be of O'Donoghue's gold-coloured Punto, was taken at 4.55pm as the vehicle was heading in the direction of Inch.

Rose Harte, mother of Robert's great friend, Heather Harte, also offered evidence as to the friendship between the two youngsters. She explained to the court that Robert, just hours before his death, looked in vain for his best friend, Heather. However, the young girl had gone to stay over with friends, and Robert was forced to play with his new BMX bike on his own, eventually calling to Wayne O'Donoghue's house where he met his death.

Rose explained the special relationship that the two children shared and how highly they both thought of Wayne O'Donoghue. 'Her [Majella's] oldest son, Robert, was very good friends with my youngest daughter, Heather, even though she was about eighteen months older than him,' Rose Harte said. 'When they were up here [in Ballyedmond] they were very close.'

Robert and Heather loved playing together and Robert would often ask to stay over at the Hartes' house. 'He stayed here on the day he bought his new mobile phone [28 December],' Rose said. 'Robert asked could he stay over and his mother said he could so long as he got his pyjamas.' But Robert, who was 'very uncomfortable' in the dark, didn't want to run down the road to his house to collect them on his own. 'Heather was teasing Robert at the door, saying he was a chicken-shit because he was afraid of the dark,' she said. But the girl then accompanied her best friend to his home – and that was to be the last night ever that Robert stayed over.

She added that both children had 'great time' for Wayne O'Donoghue who 'was the most tolerant of the three [O'Donoghue] sons to the children.' Wayne regularly took them to Midleton for sweets, ice cream and to enjoy activities like the driving range.

Mrs Harte concluded by saying that later that night, she told Heather that Robert was missing and had not returned home. 'Heather demanded to come home that [very] night. When I heard that the bike had been found in the ditch, I thought there was definitely something wrong because Robert's bike was his pride and joy,' she added.

*

It was perhaps fitting that the State case concluded with evidence as to how Robert's body had finally been discovered by Gardaí. Ivan O'Flynn, 02 Ireland engineer, explained that Gardaí had contacted the mobile phone operator about assisting in analysing the signal from the handset of the missing boy. The Gardaí contacted 02 on 10 January and the mobile phone operator immediately began reviewing every contact with Robert's handset on 4 January.

Since Robert disappeared, the handset had been inactive, and all calls to it went unanswered. Mr O'Flynn explained that 02 reviewed the handset's activity on 4 January – in particular, any movements in the location of the handset. He explained that each call that is received by a mobile phone handset is logged by a central computer and this shows the number calling, the duration of the contact and, crucially, what general area the handset is in when the call is received.

Mr O'Flynn said that every time a mobile phone leaves a general 'cell' or antenna-coverage area, it reports the fact to the general network. It was quickly noticed that Robert's mobile reported such a location shift between 4.14pm and 5.00pm on 4 January. It was noticed that Robert's handset had simultaneously reported to two cell-coverage areas, something that is relatively unusual and happened only because the signal in the area around Inch is particularly weak and the two nearest signals responded and registered the handset.

'Because the two cells don't normally interact, we could narrow down the geographic area involved,' he said. The 02 engineers, working with Garda technical experts, were able to speculate that, judging from the two cells that had reported a signal from Robert's phone, 'there was a high probability that the phone was between Aghada and Inch.' On 12 January, this confidential information was used to direct the search teams into the general Whitegate, Aghada and Inch areas. At 2.00pm that day, Robert's body was finally discovered.

CHAPTER 9: THE TRIAL CONCLUDES

FRIDAY, 9 DECEMBER 2005
THE TRIAL, DAY EIGHT

In the courtroom the sense of anticipation was palpable. After seven days of prosecution evidence in the murder trial, Wayne O'Donoghue's defence team would now open their case. Amid mounting speculation that, not surprisingly, the defendant would not take the stand himself, the defence's star witness was undoubtedly going to be Northern Ireland's State Pathologist, Prof. Jack Crane. But where was he?

As Mr Justice Carney entered the courtroom, Blaise O'Carroll SC got to his feet and explained that fog at Cork airport had delayed the flight from Belfast on which Prof. Crane was travelling. After a short recess, it was confirmed that the flight was now diverting to Farranfore in County Kerry and Prof. Crane would have to travel on to Cork by road. Defence solicitor Frank Buttimer left to meet him halfway and bring him to the court. Finally, at 2.30pm, Prof. Crane was able to begin his evidence. It emerged then too that the defence had only one other witness to call.

Prof. Crane took the stand and explained to the Court that, as well as being Northern Ireland's State Pathologist, he was also a lecturer in pathology at Queen's University in Belfast. He had been consulted by Wayne O'Donoghue's legal team and, on their behalf, had studied both Dr Cassidy's post-mortem report and the pathology photos. While he said he agreed in general with what Dr Cassidy had said, he felt there were significant areas where their emphasis differed.

'I broadly agree with the findings of Dr Cassidy. In my view this was an asphyxial type of death,' he said. But the NI pathologist said he found the lack of indicators of manual strangulation quite surprising and said that he felt the fact that Robert had been in a headlock could have been crucial. He pointed out that such headlocks are so dangerous that they can easily prove fatal even when only being used to try to subdue someone.

Prof. Crane opined that Robert might already have been dying from the effects of a headlock which, because of its accidental potency, was known to US police forces as 'a carotid sleeper'. Such types of restraining holds were once commonly used by US police forces – but, because of a number of accidental deaths, are no longer allowed. 'I don't think the wider public realise how dangerous it [a headlock] could be,' he said.

Dr Crane said he felt the most significant aspect of the pathology report was the fact that Robert had been placed in such a headlock. The pathologist explained that, when a carotid artery is blocked in such a headlock there is no guarantee that the person will revive or recover, even when the grip is released. 'He may have been in the process of dying when the neck was gripped to cause the petechial [pin-prick] haemorrhages,' he said. In general, a person's recovery is further complicated by the fact that, in such a headlock, the vagal nerve may be stimulated, effectively telling the person's heart to slow down its beating.

The vagal nerve is contained in a sheath-like structure to the side of the neck alongside critical veins and arteries. This nerve links the brain with heart-muscle function, and, when stimulated, can act to reduce a person's heart rate. It can, in certain circumstances, bring a person's heart to a virtual stop. This is believed to be a crucial factor in why such police headlocks were regarded as so dangerous in the US. Doctors are still trying to understand, he explained, why even when that pressure or stimulation is removed from the nerve, the effect can still remain. 'If you stimulate the vagal nerve you can get what we call reflex cardiac slowing. Your heart will slow and it can actually stop,' he said.

Prof. Crane said this vagal stimulation can, tragically, contribute to a person's failure to recover even when fully released from the grip. 'There is no guarantee a person will recover even when the grip is released,' he said. Prof. Crane added that he did not think that Robert was the focus of a violent assault and said that the lack of damage to Robert's throat, and the lack of signs of struggle, indicated that the force used was probably not prolonged or extreme.

He pointed out that signs of struggle are commonplace in strangulation cases although there are exceptions. But he said there were no signs of bruises or scratches to indicate that Robert had tried to struggle or fight with his assailant.

He also queried the significance attached by Dr Cassidy to bruises she found to Robert's mouth and to his ribs. 'In my view they did not play a direct part in death and again one would be just speculating to say how they were caused,' he said. Prof. Crane said such speculation, and the significance attached to the bruises, had to be weighed extremely carefully. 'We must be very careful in attributing significance to these injuries when we don't know how they occurred. They did not play a direct part in death – we simply do not know how they occurred. Again, one would just be speculating to say how they were caused,' he said.

Prof. Crane also said that, given that children bruise more easily than adults, he would have expected to find extensive bruising on Robert's chest and ribs if he had been pinned down by someone kneeling on him. The bruises to Robert's back, shoulders and buttocks could, he said, have been caused by the boy being pushed firmly back against O'Donoghue's car, or simply from falling backwards on to the ground.

None of these injuries was indicative, he said, of anything like an assault. The marks were minor and trivial.

He also focused on what he termed the relatively small number of petechial or pinprick haemorrhages found on Robert's body. In cases of asphyxia, these are the tell-tale indicators looked for by pathologists. But he said relatively few were found on Robert. In some asphyxia cases, there are so many of these petechial haemorrhages that they can actually resemble a rash on a victim's face and neck. Furthermore, he said, there was absolutely no scientific basis for saying it required fifteen to thirty seconds of asphyxial pressure to cause these petechial haemorrhages. 'We just do not know how long. What we do know is that they can occur very rapidly indeed. Vomiting or even a heavy sneeze can cause them,' he added.

Crucially, Prof. Crane said there was absolutely nothing to indicate that the boy had been subjected to a violent or prolonged assault. 'The relative lack of these signs would suggest that the force applied to the neck was not particularly severe or was not particularly prolonged,' he said. Prof. Crane also said that none of the small bones in Robert's neck were broken – again indicative of the absence of major force. Similarly, he said, none of the classic defence injuries that pathologists normally associate with cases of manual strangulation were there.

In cross-examination, Prof. Crane stated to Shane Murphy SC, for the State, that the overall pattern of injuries and marks to a body is hugely important in determining the circumstances of death. Prof. Crane acknowledged that his report was entirely based on the report of Dr Cassidy and the post-mortem photographs and he confirmed that he had not examined Robert's body in person. But Prof. Crane reiterated that he believed that Robert could have been in the process of dying as a consequence of the headlock when his neck was grabbed to cause the petechial haemorrhages.

TUESDAY, 13 DECEMBER 2005
THE TRIAL, DAY NINE
THE CONCLUSION

Geraldine O'Connell, an Xtra-vision employee from Midleton, was the second and final witness called by the defence. Her evidence focused entirely on the Nokia 3200 phone that Robert purchased on 28 December – and, importantly, the time the phone was bought. She told the court that she knew Robert for over four years. She said that he came into the Xtra-vision shop at 11.15am on 28 December to buy the mobile phone, and that he was accompanied by a young girl. As part of a promotion, the phone was on offer for €99 with a free DVD. But, because the DVD was rated '15', she told the Court she refused to give it to Robert until she rang his parents to confirm that it was all right. The timing of the phone's purchase would prove a crucial element in the trial summation now to come.

*

Shane Murphy SC, State prosecutor, got to his feet and, in just under seventy minutes, summarised the evidence of the previous eight days. Wayne O'Donoghue, he told the jury, had engaged in a pattern of concealment aimed at ensuring that critical evidence on Robert Holohan's body about how the boy had died never came to light. He told the jury they now had to consider all the evidence, and the overall pattern of what happened that day, 4 January, from which Wayne O'Donoghue was the only survivor.

'What did Wayne O'Donoghue intend to do when he applied violent force to Robert Holohan?' he asked. 'The tragedy is that Robert Holohan was a lively, active and intelligent boy who had his whole life snatched away from him,' he said. The State argued that one of the key patterns of the case was the way in which the defendant attempted, at virtually every step, to cover his tracks after Robert's death. 'There is a pattern of concealment that was engaged in by Wayne O'Donoghue,' he said, and added: 'It would suggest to you that all of this pattern of concealment demonstrates overwhelming evidence that Wayne O'Donoghue was determined to ensure that any trace of where Robert could be found, would not be found.'

Mr Murphy said that O'Donoghue's actions were emphatic. 'If Wayne O'Donoghue dug a hole on day one, he spent the next eight days very carefully filling in that hole and concealing it from the world.' He also said that a pattern of injuries to Robert's body indicated he died from asphyxia from neck compression, with indications of a headlock and manual strangulation.

Mr Murphy pointed out that O'Donoghue had given repeated false statements to Gardaí between 4 and 15 January, had taken part in the search for Robert while knowing he was dead and had even made calls to the boy's mobile phone in front of his mother. O'Donoghue also cleaned his house on 4 January to leave no trace of Robert's fatal visit – and had dumped the body in the wilderness while placing his bike so as to make Gardaí think he had been abducted.

Mr Murphy said the jury had to weigh very carefully the actions of the defendant in the hours following Robert's death, and to judge whether he had acted in a cool, controlled way or whether he was, as the defence claimed, acting in total panic. He also pointed out that, with each day Robert's body went undiscovered, damage was being done to vital evidence about how the eleven-year-old had died. He urged the jury to view (again) the video-taped interviews given by O'Donoghue to Gardaí, stressing that, in his opinion, they show someone clearly capable of controlling their emotions: 'Pay attention to his demeanour. This pattern of concealment is relevant to the overall account of Wayne O'Donoghue.' Mr Murphy reminded the jury that, when asked by Gardaí why he rang Robert's mobile when he knew the boy was already dead, O'Donoghue simply replied: 'To keep up the pretence.'

The State also contrasted the fact that the defendant was a twenty-year-old young man and Robert Holohan was an eleven-year-old boy.

The application of force in this context had to be considered very carefully.

*

In defence, Blaise O'Carroll SC vehemently disputed the State's case, claiming that the prosecution were insisting the jury consider only 'the dark side, the dark interpretation' of the evidence. He said the defendant had made 'an amazing concession' by pleading guilty to manslaughter, thus accepting full responsibility for Robert's death. He said the straightforward explanation for what had happened was that Robert died in a tragic accident, and that at no time did Wayne O'Donoghue ever *intend* to kill or seriously injure the boy.

He also raised the possibility of O'Donoghue being provoked by Robert's repeated, insistent requests to be taken to McDonald's. The boy, he said, was not on his medication for Attention Deficit Hyperactivity Disorder (ADHD) and, at such times, could be very difficult to deal with. 'Robert Holohan revered Wayne as a God-like creature – he was the big brother he didn't have,' said Mr O'Carroll. He asked the jury to contrast the cold, calculating figure the prosecution had depicted with the generous young man who used to bring Robert to McDonald's for milk-shakes, who would take him for spins in his car, who built a tree house for him and who played hurling and football with him as if with a younger brother.

O'Carroll said it was nothing short of incredible to think that Wayne O'Donoghue had ever intended any serious harm to the boy that day. 'It is completely and totally absurd: Robert, my brother, I am going to kill you; or Robert, my brother, I am going to seriously harm you,' he explained. Mr O'Carroll argued that it would be 'inconceivable' for the jury to think that the boy's death was intentional given the evidence during the trial from the two pathologists and the 'special relationship' between the twenty-year-old and the eleven-year-old boy.

He argued that Robert's death was unintentional and accidental and pointed out that even the State Pathologist, Dr Marie Cassidy, accepted that interference with the vagal nerve in the neck could have occurred. He reminded the jury that the defence's key witness, Prof. Jack Crane, said that such a headlock and vagal inteference could have been fatal for Robert – ever before a hand might have been placed on his throat.

Mr O'Carroll pointed out that there was no evidence of a violent struggle and this lent credence to the defence's claim that Robert's death was a tragic accident. And, he reminded the jury, the defendant's life had already been tremendously impacted by the awful events of last January. 'Wayne O'Donoghue had his life transformed by the incident that occurred outside his front door on 4 January. Every relationship with every human being he knows has been changed,' he said. Mr O'Carroll said that there was now 'a stain on his life' and that O'Donoghue understood that 'in a sense, it will never be the same again.'

His three-hour address to the jury concluded the summations and the next day, 14 December, the jury would be asked to deliver their verdict.

CHAPTER 10: THE VERDICT

WEDNESDAY, 14 DECEMBER 2005
THE TRIAL, DAY TEN
THE VERDICT

Mr Justice Paul Carney commenced with a detailed summary of the evidence for the jury before they began their deliberations. He focused on the key elements of the testimony and clarified legal issues arising from specific trial matters. One such issue was the prosecution's emphasis on the fact that Wayne O'Donoghue, on 16 January 2005, had described himself to two detectives as 'a murderer.' Mr Justice Carney said the jury had to decide whether this was merely a choice of words or whether the statement carried the full admission of murder as defined by the law. The summary took one hour and forty-eight minutes to deliver. The jury then had just two options open to them: either Wayne O'Donoghue was guilty of Robert Holohan's murder, or he was not. The jurors were given their issue paper and asked to reach a unanimous verdict. At twelve noon the jury went out to consider their verdict – and the agonising wait for everyone involved began.

The jury were briefly brought back to court for a few minutes on a legal issue before they resumed their deliberations. This legal issue arose after the defence requested that Mr Justice Carney re-emphasise the fact that, where two versions of events were open to the jury and they were undecided as to which was actually correct, the version that was favourable to the defendant had to be given precedence. As courtroom No. 2 emptied and the crowds dispersed, many wondered whether the verdict might even be delayed until the following day. Outside the courthouse, the Christmas celebrations were in full swing and stood in marked contrast to the sombre mood inside. News that the jury had retired to consider their verdict dominated every bulletin in the country from early morning.

By 4.00pm the jurors had been deliberating for four hours. Now, Mr Justice Carney directed that they be brought out and asked if they had yet reached a verdict. The foreperson simply told the court 'No' when asked if a decision had been reached. Mr Justice Carney said he was satisfied that sufficient deliberation had been given to the matter and he was now in a position to accept a majority verdict. However, he said he would not accept any majority below a ten-two margin.

As the jurors filed out to resume their deliberations, spectators, lawyers and media members alike exchanged glances, looked at their watches and continued their guessing-game about when a verdict would be returned. It was now 4.05pm and surely by 7.00pm the jury would be allowed to retire to a hotel and begin deliberations again the next day?

I walked out of the courtroom and pondered what to do next. I considered heading over to the *Irish Independent*'s city-centre office to start typing up some copy, ready to run back to the court at a moment's notice if necessary. But, by chance, I bumped into two colleagues and began chatting about the events of the day. Opinions varied on what was likely to happen when, at 4.20pm, a court official ran over to say that the jury had asked to return. We raced back into the court as, at 4.21pm, the jury filed back into the courtroom to confirm that they had, indeed, reached a verdict.

Mr Justice Carney sat impassive as the jury confirmed to the court official that their unanimous verdict was that Wayne O'Donoghue was not guilty of murder. As he had already pleaded guilty to Robert

Holohan's manslaughter, the only issue that now remained was the question of sentence. Seconds later, the young man had been remanded in ongoing custody to appear for sentencing before the Central Criminal Court's sitting in Ennis, County Clare, on 24 January. The seconds of shocked silence that greeted the verdict and swift remand quickly erupted into a cacophony of sobs, whispers and the bleeps of mobile phones being switched back on.

Wayne O'Donoghue held his face in his hands, concealing his emotions as the jury had returned the 'not guilty' verdict. Once again, he had maintained his bowed-head posture, but, as the verdict was confirmed, he blessed himself and partially turned in his seat to glance at his parents who were sitting behind him. As the full realisation of what had just happened dawned on him, Wayne O'Donoghue silently wept. By 5.15pm he had been led away by prison officers to await his sentence in the new year.

Mark and Majella Holohan remained seated in court as the verdict was returned, with Mark merely shaking his head and Majella tightly holding onto a photograph of her son. She had brought the simple snapshot of her beloved son into the courtroom that morning and held it against the wooden railing in front of her as if it were a talisman. Throughout the long day, the photo remained tightly grasped in her hand. In the seconds after the verdict, her shock was evident from the fact that her knuckles were almost white with the force of gripping the picture, and it was slowly bending in her hands. The Holohans – visibly upset – declined to comment to the media on the verdict.

The greatest emotion was displayed by Wayne O'Donoghue's parents, Ray and Therese. They both broke down and wept openly as the verdict was returned. Just beside them, their son's girlfriend, Rebecca Dennehy, also broke down and sobbed. Friends of the O'Donoghue family leaned over and tried discreetly to show their support and sympathy. Outside the courtroom, Ray and Therese O'Donoghue emotionally embraced their son's legal team led by Blaise O'Carroll SC, Tim

O'Leary SC and solicitor, Frank Buttimer.

The strain of the previous three weeks had taken its toll on the couple and Therese O'Donoghue sobbed uncontrollably as their son's legal team explained precisely what was going to happen next. The family, seemingly almost oblivious to their surroundings in their mixture of relief and high emotion, were surrounded by curious onlookers, reporters and photographers as everyone tried to discover what was going to happen next. Discreetly, Frank Buttimer confirmed that a statement would be made on Wayne O'Donoghue's behalf.

Ray and Therese O'Donoghue slipped away from the court, declining to comment directly to the media. However, about fifteen minutes later, Frank Buttimer, after conferring with the O'Donoghue family, walked out of the Court to address the media on the courthouse forecourt. Curious onlookers had now crowded on to Washington Street to watch what was happening, attracted by the collection of TV satellite vans, camera crews and photographers.

Facing into a wall of cameras and tape-recorders, and with a number of reporters shouting questions at him, Mr Buttimer stressed that the thoughts of everyone were now with the Holohan family and their tragic loss. He also confirmed that his client was 'very emotional' at his acquittal. 'He [Wayne] is concerned – not least for the members of the Holohan family,' he said. 'It is to be acknowledged that this has been a very difficult year for Wayne O'Donoghue and his family. But their difficulties pale to insignificance when compared to the difficulty and the sadness that have been suffered by the Holohan family over the same period of time.

'Wayne O'Donoghue's thoughts and the thoughts of his family are with the Holohans, Mark and Majella, and their family, at this point in time. Wayne O'Donoghue would like to express his gratitude to the honourable judge, Mr Justice Paul Carney, for the fair and reasonable manner in which this trial was conducted. He is deeply grateful to the jury for the attention they have given to the very, very difficult task which they have had to deal with throughout this past two and a half weeks.

'He would like to thank An Garda Síochána, the Prison Service, his legal advisors, all those in the background who have furnished advice to his legal team, to include the various medical and other personnel who have given assistance to us in the past period of time in dealing with the many difficult issues with which we have had to contend in this case. He is deeply grateful to his own family who have been there to support him throughout the entire period of this past twelve months. To all of those people who have wished him well over the past period of time, to those who have sent cards, prayers, who have contacted us by telephone, contacted Wayne through the prison service, to all of those people he is very, very grateful.'

Mr Buttimer said that his client was very much aware of all the hurt and difficulties he had caused people and deeply regretted what had happened. 'He is very aware of the difficult position in which he has placed people in regard to the circumstances of this case. From the outset, the people of Ireland have responded in a very generous and kind fashion from the time when it was necessary to commence the search right up to today. Wayne O'Donoghue is very grateful and he realises how very kind and decent people have been throughout.

'He is relieved at the verdict and he appreciates that the matter is not concluded so we will proceed to Ennis Court in January to conclude the matter. Their reaction [Wayne's parents] is that they are deeply grateful that the verdict has been recorded in the fashion that it has, and they too likewise feel very much for the Holohan family. He [Wayne] is relieved that he is not being sentenced for anything else – he will deal with the matter of sentence before Judge Carney in the appropriate fashion on the sentencing day.' When asked about how Wayne's girl-friend, Rebecca Dennehy, reacted to the verdict, Mr Buttimer said: 'I am sure that Rebecca is very relieved.'

Minutes later, Rebecca left the court, escorted by her father. She spoke briefly to reporters before being ushered away. The student said she was 'relieved' and 'delighted' by Wayne's dramatic acquittal of the murder charge. But she had found the court process exhausting, having attended the trial every day since she first gave evidence herself on the fourth day of the hearing. 'I am wrecked – really wrecked. But I am delighted with the verdict.' The student said that she now hoped to be able to speak to Wayne over the coming weeks as he prepared for his sentencing hearing in the new year.

About thirty minutes later, surrounded by Gardaí who kept photographers well back, Mark and Majella Holohan silently left the Washington Street courthouse via a side door. They simply got into a waiting car and went back to Ballyedmond. Friends explained to reporters that they just wanted to be with their children. And they wanted to be left alone. Unfortunately, it wasn't something the media was prepared to do over the next few weeks.

For several days, reporters and photographers would call to the Holohan home. They would be politely greeted and equally politely told that there would be no comment until after the Ennis sentencing hearing on 24 January. A Garda liaison officer was with the family over those traumatic days, and Supt Liam Hayes maintained daily contact with the family. It was the same story in Midleton. Camera crews, photographers, reporters and colour writers descended on the East Cork town as it found itself at the centre of an unprecedented national spotlight. Virtually every location associated with Robert was filmed and broadcast. Local politicians were interviewed about the impact on the community. Community leaders were canvassed about where they felt local sentiment would swing.

It was much the same story for Ray and Therese O'Donoghue and their other sons, Nicky and Timmy. The family had rented a house in another part of East Cork and, within twelve hours of the verdict, camera crews were parked outside their front door. Gardaí asked them to move on. Other locals made it clear they had nothing to say.

CHAPTER 11: THE FIRST ANNIVERSARY

WEDNESDAY, 4 JANUARY 2006
THE FIRST ANNIVERSARY

Mark and Majella had opted to have Robert's first anniversary Mass on the following Sunday rather than the actual date on which the anniversary fell, a Wednesday. But on 4 January, the couple included a heartbreaking memorial tribute and acknowledgement in the *Irish Examiner*, their local paper. Mark and Majella said they specifically wanted to recognise, on the anniversary of their son's death, all those who had tried so hard and so selflessly to bring him home safe to them. They said that the past year had been 'a horrific' and 'a heartbreaking and lonely time'. The couple also said that their 'fantastic family and friends' had helped them through the ordeal, together with their two children, Harry and Emma. Mark and Majella said they wanted to formally put on record their deep thanks to all those who had tried to help and comfort them in their terrible loss.

'We are incredibly grateful to all those who travelled great distances to be with us,' they wrote, 'those who comforted and supported us with food, flowers, phone calls, Mass cards, enrolments, floral tributes and personal letters. We also want to express our sincere appreciation to the thousands of people who have supported us in what has been a horrific year. We would especially wish to thank the thousands of people who came out and searched in all kinds of weather for our little boy.'

The couple specifically thanked the owners of East Cork golf club who agreed to close the facility and allow it to be transformed into the search headquarters for Robert for nine days as over three thousand volunteers combed the local countryside for the schoolboy. The Holohans also paid a moving tribute to the investigating Gardaí, led by Supt Liam Hayes, Assistant Commissioner Tony Hickey, Det. Supt John O'Mahony and Det. Sgt Peter Kenny and Det. Garda Michael O'Sullivan.

They said they were also deeply moved by the huge support the search effort for Robert attracted, with thousands of volunteers from the Civil Defence, coast- and cliff-rescue groups, sub-aqua associations, Midleton GAA club, Midleton schools, farm groups and even Cork sports stars such as Sean Óg Ó hAilpín. 'It would be impossible to thank everyone individually, but we trust this acknowledgment will be accepted as a token of our appreciation. The Holy Sacrifice of the Mass will be offered for all intentions.'

Robert's grandparents also placed a poignant poem in another local paper, the *Evening Echo*, to remember the precocious eleven-year-old who lived for his family, for his friends, for sport and for horses. It simply read:

> Falling tears and heartache
> are something we have to bear
> but losing you the way we did
> will ways seem unfair … only those who love you
> are the ones who will never forget.

Mark and Majella spent the day of 4 January quietly at home with their children, paying a private visit to Robert's grave. The only callers to their house were a few close friends and family members. But the couple were stunned by the hundreds of messages of sympathy they had received over the previous week from people they didn't know but who simply wanted the couple to know they were in their thoughts and prayers.

Throughout East Cork, there were many who also wanted to show that they hadn't forgotten Robert or the ordeal the Holohans had gone through. At Inch strand, where Robert's body was discovered, a heart-rending tribute to the boy had been built by school friends, neighbours and sympathisers. A simple wooden cross marked the isolated ditch and scrubland where Robert's body was finally discovered by searchers on 12 January 2005.

On his first anniversary, that simple wooden cross at Inch was festooned with soft toys, a miniature Santa Claus and flowers. One or two younger sympathisers had even left their own toys, as if trying, in their own innocent way, to ease the Holohans' grief. Throughout the day, people stopped at the memorial to stand in silence for a few minutes or say a few brief prayers for the little boy. I drove by myself and felt that, while it seems hard to imagine, that lonely spot actually seemed lonelier than ever.

Back in Midleton, 10.00am Mass in the Church of the Holy Rosary included a special prayer for Robert, and for Mark and Majella. A number of mourners lit candles in Robert's memory, and confirmed that, while they planned to attend Sunday's memorial mass, they just wanted to remember the boy on the exact anniversary of his death. Just yards from the church, Robert's grave was also decorated with wreaths and fresh flowers. After each Mass throughout the day, people took time to walk over to Robert's resting place and spend a few moments there. Fittingly, a few Christmas wreaths still remained in place, many from anonymous sympathisers.

SUNDAY, 8 JANUARY 2006
THE FIRST ANNIVERSARY MASS

I drove to Midleton early because, to be honest, none of us knew precisely what size crowd to expect. An indication of what the Gardaí
anticipated was evident when, just as on the day of Robert's funeral,
traffic control cones lined each side of the roadway outside the church
extending right down to the town's main street. I parked some distance
away and walked down, arriving just as the heavens opened and it
began to rain.

I huddled inside the door of the church and chatted with a few
Gardaí who were arriving to attend the anniversary Mass. There was
still half an hour to go to the ceremony and, moving inside the church, I
found a number of other reporters who had also arrived early to check
on the sermon and who was in attendance. I quickly learned that Fr
Billy O'Donovan, who had since left Midleton parish, was going to say
the Mass and deliver the keynote sermon. And virtually every Garda
officer who had been involved in the investigation would also be present to show their respect; these included Supt Liam Hayes, Det. Supt
John O'Mahony and Assistant Commissioner, Tony Hickey, who had
by now retired.

In the fifteen minutes before the Mass began, the crowds began to
stream into the church. The Holohan family took a pew just back from the
front with senior Gardaí sitting behind them. With the family's permission, the Mass was being filmed by both RTÉ and TV3. It was by now
estimated that over seven hundred people had gathered in the church.

Fr O'Donovan began by reminding people of the kind of boy Robert
was, and of how the 'candle of hope' was not extinguished when he
was buried. Instead, he assured the congregation, Robert's parents had
now become 'a beacon of hope', not just for the local community but
for the entire nation through the dignity and courage with which they
had borne their ordeal.

'Today's Mass is the first anniversary Mass for Robert Holohan and we want to welcome his parents, Mark and Majella, here today as well as their family members. And we want to especially welcome all those who, in whatever way, helped twelve months ago with the search for Robert. We gather in support of you and to pray with you.' Fr O'Donovan said that, once again, people were drawn to the church by the need to pray.

'It is a year ago – and maybe here today we need to take our cue from you, Mark and Majella and family. In the past twelve months you have shown remarkable courage and strength. You have been an example under extraordinarily difficult circumstances. The fourth of January was the first anniversary of Robert's death – and the first anniversary is a special and a significant time. In that first year there are so many firsts: his birthday, Christmas, holidays, going back to school, matches, fishing, pony club and the many other family occasions that have come and gone in that year. But Robert wasn't there. The pain of the first year is the most difficult time.'

Fr O'Donovan said that the pain of the family was shared by the whole community. 'Today we pray for you – that it may not be so difficult in the future. Today, we look back on the past year. Your family has been remarkable in the last twelve months. Maybe today you are asked to continue to be a beacon of light and of hope for the future.'

Poignantly, Fr O'Donovan pointed out that the first anniversary Mass was taking place on the exact date that, the previous year, the town of Midleton had lit a candle of hope for Robert's safe return as the search effort for him reached its peak. He said it was significant that, even when Robert's body was discovered on 12 January, that the candle of hope had not been extinguished. 'We lit a candle of hope for Robert right here in front of this altar, and that candle burned around the clock. The candle was not put out when Robert was found and it continued to burn through his funeral Mass and for many weeks afterwards. It was, during those weeks, a powerful beacon of hope for the future.

'Now you [the Holohans] as a family must seek to go forward, and you as a community here in Midleton must seek to go forward. As a family and as a community, we must never forget Robert.' Fr O'Donovan also urged people to remember 'the extraordinary response from the community and the nation' that Robert's disappearance provoked. 'We rediscovered, even if for a brief time, human and Christian values that many thought had been missing.'

The Offertory gifts were then brought up by Mark and Majella while their daughter, Emma, read one of the Prayers of the Faithful. Her simple words were used by numerous newspapers the following day to sum up the mood of the day in Midleton. The pretty, blonde nine-year-old stepped up to the lectern, which was almost too tall for her, and simply explained: 'Harry and I miss Robert so much.'

Outside, after Mass, the weather had brightened and the Holohans lingered to thank people for attending. Reporters chatted with both the Holohans and the Gardaí, and everyone's mind was concentrated on an Ennis courtroom just sixteen days away.

CHAPTER 12: THE SENTENCING HEARING

TUESDAY, 24 JANUARY 2006
THE SENTENCING HEARING

Tuesday, 24 January 2006 dawned bright and dry in Ennis, County Clare. Locals on their way to work knew that something unusual was happening in the town from the congestion around Ennis's magnificent and recently restored courthouse. From 7.00am, reporters and photographers began to gather outside the imposing court, some to grab space for their TV vans, others just to ensure they didn't miss any photo opportunities. The tall, column-lined façade was tailor-made as a backdrop for live TV broadcasts, and TV stations, including RTÉ, TV3 and TG4, came prepared, with outside broadcast vans and double camera crews for additional reporting.

By 11.00am, when the Central Criminal Court session was about to begin, such was the throng of reporters, camera crews, photographers and TV researchers that special arrangements had to be made. Gerry Curran of the Court Service arranged that once a jury panel had been dispensed with for a separate murder trial beginning that day in Ennis, the media, now over fifty strong, would be shepherded down from an overhead balcony into the courtroom proper for the sentencing hearing.

As reporters filed noisily into the court, Mark and Majella Holohan sat to the right of the wood-panelled room. Directly facing Mr Justice Paul Carney was the defendant, Wayne O'Donoghue, who adopted his usual pose of sitting, shoulders hunched, eyes downcast to the floor. Dressed in a dark suit, the young man once again appeared heavier and paler than the twenty-year-old who first made headlines the previous January. He was flanked by prison guards. Directly behind O'Donoghue sat his parents, Ray and Therese, and his girlfriend, Rebecca Dennehy, who was accompanied by her father.

The sentencing hearing began with Chief Supt Liam Hayes, who had led the investigation into Robert's disappearance, taking the stand. He confirmed that, after his 16 January statement, Wayne O'Donoghue had been co-operative with the Gardaí. He also acknowledged that, prior to killing Robert, O'Donoghue had been of good behaviour with no convictions of any kind. Supt Hayes then finished his brief submission by acknowledging that it 'could be years' before the Holohan family recovered from the trauma of their son's death.

*

Seconds later, Majella Holohan was called to address the court and deliver her Victim Impact Statement to the hearing. Any murmur of conversation in the packed courtroom faded as Majella, with a brief nod of support from her husband, Mark, took the stand. The anticipation was palpable as the she settled herself in the witness box and looked at the judge for permission to begin her submission.

She opened by thanking all the people who had offered to help her prepare her crucial submission to the court. 'But,' she began to read from her notes, slowly and carefully at first, her voice gaining in confidence as she read, 'I think only a mother who has lost a child will know exactly what to say,' she explained as she held up her eleven-page, hand-written note. Her hand trembled slightly as she held the pages, clearly numbered in the top right corner to help her keep track as she read her submission.

'I am Majella Holohan, mother of Robert Holohan. I have been married to Mark for the last fifteen years. We had three children – Rob was our first-born. He was eleven-years-old when he died. We have two other children, Emma and Harry.

'After Harry was born I became a full-time home maker and occupied myself looking after my family and providing for them as best I could. Our life revolved around our children and we had an idyllic rural life and we were a very happy family. Rob was our pride and joy. In all the hundreds of letters I received over the last year people have commented on what a beautiful-looking child he was. He *was* a beautiful child and I mean that in relation to his physical appearance and his nature. From the moment Robert was born he brought enormous joy to my husband and I; indeed my parents, William and Mona – for our families, Rob was a character.

'Rob had a lot of friends through school, the GAA and the pony club. He loved the outdoor life and before he owned his own pony he mucked out at local stables and took riding lessons. He loved all animals and used to help my father with his greyhounds. He had his own dog, Taz, a beautiful Labrador. After school, Rob would be over at the horses. He loved it. He would come home filthy and exhausted, but always looking forward to the next day.

'After about two years we decided that this was indeed more than a whim, so we bought Rob his own pony. You would think we had paid thousands for her and that she was a famous horse. He was thrilled with her and decided to call her Stella. Rob groomed her and kept his saddle and bridle spotless. Every photo was of Rob hugging Stella. Once a year Rob helped out at a camp for the mentally handicapped and gave children spins on his pony; most of you probably read this in the newspapers.

'He had a good nature – he gave up his bedroom and slept in the guest bedroom when I took several Chernobyl children in the summer. He told me, on a trip to EuroDisney, that Space Mountain was easy. He laughed as I closed my eyes – I was petrified. One day, when I wasn't feeling well, he made scrambled eggs and tea – but he had added too much salt. But as mothers do, I ate it all up. Rob was not very academic but with private grinds in English to help with his dyslexia he was well able to keep up with his class. He was a brilliant swimmer and has a lot of certificates for swimming. Anyone that calls to our house is amazed at his lovely art work.

'Rob had a diagnosis of ADHD and dyslexia, a condition that I suffer from myself. I don't regard it as a stigma. We sought the best advice possible, including advice from a private educational psychologist and a private child psychiatrist. Rob had medication to ameliorate the adverse effects of the ADHD and, as far as we were concerned, the condition was controlled and he was a happy, outgoing child.

'We had plans for Rob's future education, including sending him to Midleton College. We had planned for his future. Mark and I had made wills in which we had left our family home to Rob. Parenting can be difficult and you start at the beginning with sleepless nights and so on, but, as our child got older, he blossomed and we were looking forward to a future with Rob. My husband, Mark, is interested in outdoor activities and sports and he spent a lot of time with Rob. He looked forward to doing so in the future. Mark enjoyed taking him fly-fishing and doing the things that fathers do with their sons.

'We felt secure living in the rural area where we did. We felt secure in letting Rob visit with his immediate neighbours, including the O'Donoghue family. If Rob had to go anywhere, we would, of course, drive him and collect him. However, we felt that it was safe for him to call on his nextdoor neighbour. We did not have the slightest suspicion in relation to his friendship with Wayne O'Donoghue. You cannot – and should not – keep one's children in a glass cage. One has to let them develop and form relationships. If one is overprotective, one's children will never be able to stand on their own two feet.

Right: Stuffed animals and toys lie by the cross marking the spot where the remains of Robert Holohan were found near Inch Strand.

Below: Austin Bolger, owner of Dennehy's shop in Midleton, closes his shop as a mark of respect to the Holohan family during Robert's funeral.

As a mark of respect to the Holohan family,

This shop will remain closed for the duration of the funeral of Robert Holohan

Above: An aerial photo of the attendance outside Holy Rosary Church, Midleton for the funeral of Robert Holohan.

Right: Majella Holohan at the funeral of her son.

Above: Robert's parents, Mark and Majella Holohan, with his coffin during his funeral.

Below: Mourners outside Holy Rosary Church, attending Robert's funeral.

Above: Mourners pray in remembrance at the grave of Robert Holohan at the Holy Rosary cemetery, Midleton.

Below: Wayne O'Donoghue being led into Midleton Court.

Left: Rebecca Dennehy, girlfriend of Wayne O'Donoghue at Cork Courthouse.

Below: Frank Buttimer, Wayne O'Donoghue's solicitor, addressing the press outside the Central Criminal Court in Cork. Writer and reporter, Ralph Riegel pictured to the right of Mr Buttimer.

Right: Ray and Therese O'Donoghue, Wayne O'Donoghue's parents, outside Cork Courthouse.

Below: The grave of eleven-year-old Robert Holohan at the Holy Rosary cemetery.

ROBERT HOLOHAN

AGED 11 YEARS

REST IN PEACE

Above: Mark, Harry, Emma and Majella Holohan pictured at Robert Holohan's Memorial Mass in the Holy Rosary Church.

'My husband and I have known Wayne O'Donoghue and his family for the past ten years since we first moved into our house in Ballyedmond. Rob adored Wayne and looked up to him like an older brother. We trusted Wayne completely. From when Rob was a young age, six or seven, he used to play games with Wayne – soccer, make tree houses etc. There was a nine-year age gap between Wayne and Rob. The age gap never seemed to bother Wayne. When Wayne's previous car was burned out at the place of his employment, Rob was very upset about this. He cried and he wanted to contribute money from his own small savings to enable Wayne to purchase a new car. This is how he felt about Wayne.

'Our lives changed utterly and dramatically on 4 January 2005. Rob and I had our lunch together at around 1.15pm. He was delighted with his medal, which he had got the night before at a GAA presentation. He spoke of the *craic* he had with his friends and his love of hurling. He said in future he would give "half-and-half" to horse-riding and hurling practice.

'After his lunch he went out on his new bike which he got for Christmas. He built a ramp out on the drive and I watched as he sped over it, laughing. After coming in again, he went back out again and went out the drive on his bike. That was the last time I was to see my beautiful little boy. I rang him at about 3.30pm and it rang out. I rang again at 3.45pm and Rob's phone went on to the messaging machine. After ringing a few more times, I sent my daughter, Emma, down to O'Donoghue's house to see if Rob was there. That is how much confidence I had in the safety of the rural area that I felt safe in sending my eight-year-old daughter next door to collect her older brother.

'I telephoned neighbours to check if Rob was there. I telephoned the O'Donoghue household and Wayne answered the phone. Wayne O'Donoghue told me that he hadn't seen Rob since 2.15pm. I had a normal conversation with him. As word spread of the fact that Rob was missing, neighbours and Gardaí called. At around 9.30pm Wayne

O'Donoghue, his two brothers and his father called. Wayne sought to reassure me and told me not to worry, that Rob would be found and he would be all right. In my presence, he telephoned Rob's mobile phone and told me that there was no answer.

'I rang Rob's mobile phone a couple of times and left messages like: "Rob, this is Mam, please phone me." Later that evening, Rob's bike was found and the Gardaí wanted somebody to identify it. I asked Wayne O'Donoghue if he would be able to identify it and he did. He returned to the house and told me that it was Rob's bike. To realise that your child is missing is a nightmare. I prayed and prayed that Rob would return home that night. We remained up all night in the company of the Gardaí. The following days and nights during the search were a living hell for us all. Trying to keep our composure in front of Harry and Emma was very difficult. Breaking down, they watching us crying, they waking up at night, crying, looking for Rob and being inconsolable. The horrendous thoughts that were going through my mind wondering where Rob was being kept, the terrible things that were being done to him.

'There were also numerous rumours and innuendo about our family – all of which were completely false. These hurt terribly, as did the fact that Wayne O'Donoghue intimated to the Gardaí that he heard screams from our house and that Mark used to more than beat Rob. The only screams that were heard from our home were the screams of joy and happiness. Mark only chastised Rob the same as any normal father would. These were mean and nasty suggestions to make. He also said I couldn't cope – this from a man who strangled a child and tried to blame the child. I stayed at home each day in case Rob would come in. I kept ringing him on his mobile phone, but there was no answer. I knew that Rob was terrified of the dark and I was afraid for him. The days and the nights got longer and longer. The lack of sleep, the anxiety, the frustration that he was not being found, the utter despair. The depth of pain was unbelievable.'

Majella broke down and sobbed audibly as she recalled the agony they had been put through by their next-door neighbour.

'All this could have been avoided if Wayne just made an anonymous phone-call. On one of these days I recall seeing Wayne walking past our house. I knocked on the window and beckoned him to come over to the house. He jumped the ditch, came up and I said to Wayne that it was desperate about poor Rob. I observed that Rob had loved Wayne. He just nodded his head. I asked him to come in for a cup of tea, but he declined as he said his boots were dirty. I told him he was doing 'too much' searching. He walked back down the lane. I still cannot believe how he was able to face me that day in my own kitchen, so bare-faced, when he knew that he had killed my poor boy and had dumped his body in black bin-liners in a ditch at Inch. I feel he was so cunning and devious to be able to look me straight in the face and ask me had we any news on Rob. I don't know how anybody could be so deceitful.

'Then to be told that Rob had been found dead after some eight days searching. Our eleven-year-old beautiful son, that he was dumped in a ditch. It was a miracle that he was found at all. The scene at Inch was a wilderness – that was why his perfect little body was so badly damaged that we could not see him, could not hug him or hold him to say goodbye. To my horror, I discovered that his little body was to be left out overnight until the State Pathologist visited the scene the following day. You wouldn't do it to a dog.

'One cannot imagine how any mother or father would feel to learn that their child's body was to be left out in the wild overnight and the weather was so bad. I thought that we may get his body back on the following day but it was not until the Friday that it was returned to us. When the hearse came to our house the little white coffin was sealed. All we got was a lock of Rob's hair. This could have been avoided too if that phone-call was made.' She sobbed again before continuing.

'On the day that we got Rob's body back, I remember looking out the window and seeing Wayne walking his dog in the lane between our two houses. I knocked on the window to catch his attention. Wayne put his head down and kept walking. I wanted to ask him to say one of the Prayers of the Faithful at Rob's funeral. Wayne never looked up, and I thought nothing of it at the time. I first presumed that he did not hear me. It is fortunate that I didn't speak to him because I would hate it now to think of Wayne having any act or part in Rob's funeral.

'I cannot get out of my mind the image of the body of my precious, beautiful boy, Rob, being dumped at a ditch in Inch. He was only eleven-years-old and left to the elements for nine days. You wouldn't do it to a dog. Having to tell my daughter, Emma, who was eight, was one of the most horrible experiences that I have ever faced. I tried as best I could to explain to Harry, then aged four, that his older brother was dead.

'They could not comprehend that Wayne had killed Rob, Wayne being his friend. They both had to have counselling. Emma still cries a lot and Harry still doesn't understand. He still calls out for Rob and both ask a lot of questions about death and heaven, and where is Rob gone?

'To bury your child is a nightmare but to bury him in these circumstances is impossible to describe – the depth of despair, the utter hopelessness, the injustice that was done to Rob and ourselves. The day at Rob's funeral was surreal. People turned out in their thousands and were extremely supportive. The ceremony was beautiful but heartbreaking – what made it worse for us was that the suspicion was on us and on everyone that we knew. The truth was Rob's killer was still on the loose and we had no idea as to what had happened to Rob. I worried were Emma and Harry safe. I felt as if my whole life was falling apart. Who would do such a thing: kill an innocent child and let it go on for so long?

'Rob was everything to me and I loved him so much. He reminded me of myself more so than my other two children. In 2004 he was in Croke Park, wearing his red-and-white jersey, supporting Cork. His favourite player was Sean Óg Ó hAilpín. The 2005 final between Cork and Galway was emotional. I couldn't watch it, thinking that Robert should be there with us, watching his favourite team win and his favourite player lift the cup.

'Other special occasions – such as birthday parties, Christmas – which were family times of joy and closeness are now times of tears and sorrow. The fact that Rob was killed so close to our family home is very hard to cope with. We will have to sell. Each day I pass the location where it happened. This brings questions into my head like: Why did he die? Did he scream? If he did why didn't I hear him? Could I have done something? Did he suffer much?'

Majella paused and wept. She took a deep breath, gazed around the courtroom and then, clearly steeling herself, plunged the hearing into sensation. 'Our doctors told us to try and get on with our lives. But how can we, knowing there was semen found on my son's body?' she demanded. Referring to the defendant's claim that the fatal row between Robert and Wayne erupted over thrown stones, Majella disputed the allegation. 'Forensic examination could not find any stone marks on the [Fiat] car. If this was an accident, why didn't Wayne call? Why were there no fingerprints found on Robert's phone – not even his own? Who wiped it clean and deleted the images on it?'

Mrs Holohan also claimed that two 999 emergency calls were logged to her son's mobile phone in the days before his death. 'Why did my little boy ring 999 later that morning as the phone records show he did?' She also asked why a twenty-year-old would be ringing an eleven-year-old boy at 6.00am and why her son was in the defendant's bedroom on another morning. 'What was Robert going to Wayne's bedroom for at 7.30am when he was supposed to be on a sleepover?' She also asked why her son was found with both of his shoes off at Inch Strand.

Majella paused, sobbed softly and wiped the tears from her eyes as the courtroom sat in stunned silence.

The eight questions she had raised left the courtroom in shock. It subsequently emerged that the questions levelled in the thirty-second conclusion to her Victim Impact Statement were not included in the written summary shown to both the court and the defence before the hearing. Within seconds of Mrs Holohan concluding her statement in sobs of distress, Blaise O'Carroll SC, for the defence, had risen to object and to ask Mr Justice Carney for a brief adjournment. A request for a recess was immediately granted and the courtroom emptied as journalists ran to file copy and photographers moved to take up position on the courtroom steps.

*

The shock at the implications of what had just been said was tangible, and the silence of the courtroom was sundered by a wall of noise from the corridor outside as reporters spoke to their news-desks, shocked members of the public exchanged whispered views and supporters of both families conducted hushed exchanges.

Just over twenty minutes later, Mr Justice Carney resumed the hearing, only to be informed by Mr O'Carroll that his client's name had been 'blackened and traduced beyond hope of repair.' The defence team objected that they had not been made aware of the concluding matters introduced to the court by Mrs Holohan. Even allowing for high emotions it was pointed out that these issues dramatically impacted on Wayne O'Donoghue.

The court was then told that, because of what had happened, the defence were now not prepared to offer any further evidence or call any witnesses. It subsequently emerged that the witnesses earmarked to offer testimony included Wayne O'Donoghue, who wanted to personally apologise for his actions and explain the tragic events of 4 January. The other witnesses were to include Wayne's father, Ray, a consultant psychiatrist Dr Brian McCaffrey, and Wayne's former teacher, Denis Ring, principal of Midleton CBS.

Mr Justice Carney replied that he was a professional judge and would impose sentence on the matters brought before him in evidence and absolutely nothing else. He was assured by the defence legal team that they retained 'full confidence' in Ireland's most experienced criminal law judge. But it didn't change the fact that the defence would not now offer the evidence that they had originally planned.

*

Turning to Majella Holohan, now seated in the body of the court and clutching her husband's hand, the judge warned her to brace herself for what was about to happen. 'The sentence in this case is going to disappoint you,' he bluntly admitted.

Mr Justice Carney paused before addressing the full court: 'I want to say unequivocally at the outset that I am dealing with a manslaughter and not with a cover-up. A manslaughter has been described as the most elastic of crimes because the penalty can range from a suspended sentence to one of life imprisonment. It is now my function to select a punishment at or between these extremes and explain my reasons to the nation and to the Holohan family as best I can. I will be doing so on the basis of the evidence presented in open court and no other consideration.

'In this case, evidence was given by pathologists on each side. For the prosecution, evidence was given by the State Pathologist, Dr Marie Cassidy, and for the defence, evidence was given by the Chief Pathologist for Northern Ireland, Prof. Jack Crane. They were in broad agreement, with some difference in emphasis. The evidence of both pathologists was to the effect that the injuries on Robert's body were light.

'I find of particular significance that Prof. Crane went on to say that the injuries were consistent with those which resulted from a restraining technique employed by several police forces in the US. When it became apparent that this technique was causing unexpected deaths, its authorised use was terminated. This evidence suggests to me that the injuries we are concerned with here were at the horse-play end of the scale.

'After the death, the cover-up was appalling. There can be no excusing what was done. There can be no mitigating of what was done. The cover-up caused incredible grief and distress to the Holohan family. It permitted of the body being mutilated by animals, it tied up the emergency forces of the State over a protracted period and caused the people of Ireland as a whole to join in the Holohans' grief. It cannot be dismissed as being due to panic by reason of the calculation and deliberation involved.

'I am not punishing the accused expressly in respect of the cover-up, although it comes into play as part of the impact on the victims and I take it into account in that regard. I must bear in mind, however, that it could have formed the basis of substantive charges and they were not laid.

'After the funeral, matters changed. The accused confessed to his father what he had done. His father immediately locked him in a shed to prevent self-harm and sent for the family's solicitor. The family's solicitor said this was a matter way beyond his experience and competence and Mr Frank Buttimer must be sent for. This approach on the part of the family's solicitor was absolutely the correct and appropriate one. Mr Buttimer arrived immediately and tendered his advice. As a result, the accused, prior to arrest, dictated a seven-and-a-quarter hour confession. He refused breaks which he was offered and carried on until the completion of his confession.

'He then sought an opportunity to see his girlfriend to tell her face-to-face what he had done. The O'Donoghue family sought an opportunity to face the Holohans but were advised against this by the guards. They then vacated their family home so as to avoid unnecessary distress being occasioned to the Holohans and they have remained away ever since. I am satisfied that from the point when the accused first confessed to his father, genuine remorse was in play.

'It is common for family members at the conclusion of cases such as this to complain that the life of their loved one was valued by the court only at the level of the sentence imposed. This is an approach which the courts do not and cannot take. Obviously, young Robert's life was so precious as to be incapable of measurement in any such terms. It is also the case that nothing I can do or say could in any way assuage the Holohans' grief.'

Mr Justice Carney said that he was 'not a free agent' when it came to sentencing, but stressed that the terms he imposed must not concern themselves with revenge or retaliation, must offer the accused some hope for the reconstruction of his life and must also reflect the fact that many previous manslaughter sentences had been 'decimated' by the Court of Criminal Appeal.

'I take account, of course, of the effect of the crime on the Holohan family. I take account of the accused being of previously good character. It would be my expectation that he would not re-offend, particularly having regard to the evidence I heard during the trial, although Mr O'Carroll is refusing to offer me any evidence today of the continuing and ongoing support of his girlfriend, Rebecca. I take account of the fact that at all times he pleaded guilty to what he was ultimately convicted of. Balancing all these factors as best as I humanly can, I sentence the accused to four years' imprisonment to date from the date of his arrest,' he concluded.

With that, on the thirteenth day of the case, Mr Justice Carney concluded the proceedings and left the courtroom. But, almost as if held in abeyance until his departure, as soon as the door to the judge's chamber slowly began to close, the courtroom exploded in a flurry of controversy. If anyone thought that the sentencing hearing would end the drama over Robert Holohan's killing, they were emphatically to be proved wrong.

CHAPTER 13: THE SENTENCE – REACTION

TUESDAY, 24 JANUARY 2006
REACTION

The words of Mr Justice Carney were still echoing around the Ennis courtroom when the fall-out began. Mark and Majella Holohan looked visibly shocked as the full realisation of the four-year jail term sank home. Majella leaned forward in her seat, obviously distraught, and stared across the room at her son's killer. 'We will appeal it, we will appeal it,' she insisted as Wayne O'Donoghue was quickly led out of the room by two prison guards.

Mark Holohan – his face flushed – initially just slumped forward and held his head in his hands. Then he shook his head in disbelief before slowly standing up, fists clenched to his side. Raising his eyes to the courtroom roof, almost in protest at what he'd just heard, he expressed his shock at the four-year sentence.

The lay-out of the Ennis courtroom required the prison guards to usher O'Donoghue out via the rear of the seats which were occupied by the Holohan family and the Gardaí. Still visibly enraged, Mark Holohan turned to stare at his son's killer and shouted at his retreating back: 'You're a disgrace, boy.' He then turned and glared back across the courtroom at O'Donoghue's girlfriend, Rebecca Dennehy, who was still sitting beside Wayne's parents, Ray and Therese, and demanded: 'Are you going to marry him now?'

Rebecca Dennehy immediately broke down in tears and, with her father's arm around her shoulders, was then escorted, sobbing, from the courtroom. Minutes later, her father took her out of the court building to a waiting car. Both father and daughter remained stoically silent as they moved through the waiting media throng, refusing even to acknowledge questions shouted at them. They quickly sat in their car and drove away, ignoring the photographers who filmed their every move.

The fall-out from the sentence was continuing to escalate. Photographers waited near both front and rear exits from the courthouse while reporters hovered inside, waiting to see if a rumoured press conference with the Holohans would materialise. It was a scene of total confusion. Reporters rushed to check with their news-desks and legal advisers about the implications of what Majella Holohan had just said. Because of the timing involved, several stations opted not to use the word 'semen' in their initial lunchtime summaries of the sentencing hearing. However, that would change as the day wore on.

Inside the court premises, journalists waited in anticipation of what would happen next. The Court Service had made arrangements for a special area to be provided in case the Holohan family wanted to address the media. But, just as in the verdict of the Central Criminal Court jury on 14 December, the first to break the silence was Wayne O'Donoghue's solicitor, Frank Buttimer. The Cork criminal law specialist strode out the front door of the courthouse and walked slowly down the steps of the building to a fenced area where the TV crews and photographers waited. For those not already in place, there was a frantic scramble to tape his words.

Mr Buttimer, dressed in a light-brown pinstripe suit, began by thanking the courts and Mr Justice Carney for the fair and balanced manner in which the trial was conducted.

'Wayne O'Donoghue and his family are relieved these legal proceedings have now been concluded. He is grateful to his Honour, Mr Justice Paul Carney, and previously to the jury for the care and attention they have given to these very, very difficult matters. He and his family repeat an expression of sympathy to Mark and Majella Holohan and their family. Wayne O'Donoghue would very much like to thank most sincerely all of the people who have expressed support, sympathy, care and concern for him throughout these very difficult times.

'On the last occasion I said that he accepted that he had put people into a very difficult position because of the facts of this particular case. He understands that. However, he is deeply grateful to the people who expressed understanding to him for the difficulties he has faced in relation to these matters. In today's proceedings certain matters were raised by Majella Holohan concerning the conduct of the investigation and that of the trial and the suggestion is that there was certain evidence that was not led by the prosecution. As far as the defence is concerned, all relevant evidence available to the prosecution was led and indeed was led properly by the prosecution.

'Indeed, the defence is of the view, and confirms, that nothing relevant was withheld or concealed from the jury in any fashion whatsoever or deemed inadmissible by his Honour, Mr Justice Carney, during his conduct of the trial. Wayne O'Donoghue from day one, that is 16 January when he came forward, has accepted responsibility for the tragic death of Robert Holohan. He accepts the penalty of the courts and he will now proceed to serve his sentence without appeal.'

But, almost as soon as the solicitor had concluded his remarks, he was swamped by a barrage of questions about the sensational matters that Majella Holohan had just raised in court.

Questioned repeatedly about the discovery of semen on Robert's body, Mr Buttimer repeated his insistence that his client was not involved in any type of impropriety. 'Wayne denies any impropriety of any kind with regard to that. I repeat, all relevant evidence was led by the prosecution. This trial was conducted quite properly.' Mr Buttimer insisted that questions of DNA were not for the defence to answer. 'It is not a matter for Wayne O'Donoghue to do anything other than to plead guilty to the manslaughter, which he has done. The trial was conducted properly.'

Mr Buttimer did acknowledge that his client was 'relieved' at the sentence that was imposed, and was now ready to serve the time the Court required of him.

'I found it difficult to get a word with him afterwards but he is relieved that the sentence is as it is. He accepts the penalty of the court and according to my understanding, that is the conclusion for Wayne O'Donoghue. I believe his family are relieved that the proceedings are over. I think it is a balanced and fair sentence. It is fair and reasonable.' When questioned about the emotional scenes at the end of the sentencing hearing, Mr Buttimer said his client understands that feelings were running high. 'He understands that there is a high degree of emotion, but those matters are for the Holohans to deal with.'

Declining to answer further shouted queries, Mr Buttimer went back to confer with the O'Donoghue family. Less than an hour later, Mark and Majella Holohan, escorted by Gardaí, left the Ennis courthouse by the rear exit and declined to comment to the waiting media. Majella Holohan, her husband supporting her by the arm, paused as she recognised a few faces amongst the gathered reporters.

'It has been an horrendous year,' she said. 'I would like to thank the searchers who brought our little boy back to us. I hope that you will respect our privacy now to grieve for poor old Rob. We will never forget him. I would like to thank you all for your help in the search for Rob. Otherwise he would still be lying in a ditch at Inch. Thanks very much,' Majella said. Mark Holohan declined to comment on any potential appeal, clearly determined to get his family away from the mêlée of the Ennis media. 'I don't want to comment on it at the moment, if you don't mind.'

The couple then got into a waiting car and drove back to Ballyedmond to be with their children. I stood in the car park and wondered what was going to happen next. Majella's statement had stunned everyone. But, once again, time became an issue and I had to head to the Ennis hotel where most of the media pool had set up workstations, including my colleagues Kathy Donaghy, Miriam Lord and Eugene Hogan. Luckily, we were able to secure printed versions of both Mr Justice Carney's sentencing statement and the hand-written statement of Majella Holohan. Pointedly, her written statement ended without the thirty seconds or so conclusion to her address and its eight dramatic questions.

And with that, the courthouse began to empty, save for the TV outside broadcast units which would use the courthouse as a backdrop for live bulletins which began at 5.30pm and continued until 9.00pm. The story had proved to be even more sensational that many had expected. The sentencing hearing was the main story on every TV and radio station in Ireland that night. It dominated the front page of every newspaper produced in Ireland, not just the next day but for the entire week. Even the Sunday newspapers, produced five days later, were still delving into the implications of Majella Holohan's actions, the merits of the four-year sentence and the implications for future Victim Impact Statements.

That night, TV3 ran a phone poll on their main news bulletin about the length of the sentence handed down to Wayne O'Donoghue, and eighty-four percent of callers felt that it was too lenient. Three days later, a *Sunday Independent* phone poll indicated that seventy-seven percent of respondents were not happy with the outcome of the case, and sixty-eight percent said they believed that the Director of Public Prosecutions should explain, at least to the Holohan family, why apparently crucial DNA evidence was omitted from the trial.

THE FALL-OUT

The furore over the four-year sentence and the Victim Impact Statement was explored in the media throughout the remainder of the week. Pat Kenny on 'The Late Late Show' staged a special debate on crime and sentencing policy where I was asked to recount the court proceedings as part of a panel discussion. 'Questions & Answers' staged a special debate on the matter, where Frank Buttimer addressed the issues raised by Majella Holohan. The solicitor spoke again on RTÉ's 'Morning Ireland' and 'News At One' programmes on Radio One as well as on various local radio stations. Hardly surprisingly, the newspapers that Wednesday, 25 January, were dominated by Majella Holohan's claims about semen found on her son's body.

It transpired that a DNA test conducted by an overseas consulting forensic laboratory was at the centre of Majella Holohan's statements. This fact dominated the front page of every newspaper in the State including both the *Irish Independent* and *The Irish Times*. The papers revealed that, on 13 January, shortly after Robert's body was moved back to CUH, the State Pathologist, Dr Marie Cassidy, took various sample swabs for analysis. One such swab was taken from Robert's hand.

I learned from Garda sources that when this swab was analysed it was found to contain minute traces of semen. These were examined in detail by a respected consulting forensic laboratory and subjected to various DNA analyses. One of these crucial tests was called Low Copy Number (LCN). This state-of-the-art test is increasingly relied upon by police forces throughout Europe and North America because, unlike other older DNA tests, it can be conducted even with minute samples. Often an LCN test can be conducted on samples containing merely a few cells.

The sample from Robert was cross-referenced with various samples provided by the Gardaí as a result of their investigation.

The initial LCN test – which was entirely based on the Inch sample – offered a one-in-70-million chance that the DNA sample originated from someone other than Wayne O'Donoghue.

However, that provisional analysis came before further tests were conducted on other submitted samples. As part of the exhaustive Garda investigation, samples had also been taken from the mat in the bathroom of the O'Donoghues' Ballyedmond home. It emerged that semen samples were also found on this mat. The bathroom mat had been on the floor when Robert Holohan's body had been laid on the ground by Wayne O'Donoghue.

Crucially, the two DNA samples – from Inch and from the Ballyedmond mat – both underwent analysis under the LCN technique and the results forced the original, preliminary analysis to be withdrawn. Ultimately, the forensic scientists were not able to offer any definitive verdict on the identity of the Inch semen. Tests conducted at the behest of the defence legal team indicated that the semen found at Inch was not that of Wayne O'Donoghue. That forensic report – compiled by a respected UK team – suggested that the presence of semen at the scene in Inch was caused by accidental cross-transfer from the bathroom mat.

Ultimately, the two-week Central Criminal Court trial was not asked to consider any DNA material from either the State or the defence legal teams. The State made no attempt to introduce such evidence, and it was not brought before Mr Justice Carney in the form of legal argument.

It also emerged that Wayne O'Donoghue, after having initially told detectives that there was no way they would find semen on Robert's body, said that the DNA material they were referring to must have originated from a towel or mat that was in the bathroom at the time the boy's body was laid on the floor.

It was against this backdrop that Frank Buttimer gave a number of high-profile radio interviews over the following days. In one interview, on RTÉ Radio One with Marian Finucane, he insisted the DNA material found at Inch had nothing whatsoever to do with Wayne O'Donoghue.

In answer to several questions Mr Buttimer said that the State was already 'rowing back' on its initial forensic findings when the defence experts delivered their own analysis. 'It was abundantly clear that there was a comprehensive answer to any suggestion that forensic material was in any way linked to Wayne O'Donoghue. They [the experts] came to a conclusion that was completely favourable to the defence. I have no doubt that it was [semen] but it was not my client's. If it was evidential material in the prosecution of Wayne O'Donoghue, it would have been introduced as part of the trial.'

But the single most detailed interview the solicitor gave was on Cork local radio station, 96FM, the day after the sentencing hearing. Mr Buttimer addressed each of the eight issues that Robert's mother had raised over a period of more than forty-five minutes. In a sometimes heated interview with presenter, Neil Prendeville, Frank Buttimer insisted that his client was shocked by the virulence of the tabloid media coverage, and he was himself taken aback by some of the inaccuracies in the coverage.

'One station made a comment on their programme that was factually incorrect. I took issue with it and rang them, and [said] that I would be dealing with their material,' he said. The coverage had left the entire defence team horrified. 'It's tough enough to have to take this on the chin … but for there to be this suggestion out there that there is [another] element to it is way over the top. It is wrong. It is factually incorrect, unsustainable and action will be taken.'

Mr Buttimer said that elements of the media were now determined to conduct a re-trial of the case, with all the hurt and anguish involved. 'The problem is the one issue which was not evidential, the forensic matter [the semen]. We clearly take issue with that. People out there should understand that if there was any question of linking such material with an accused person in a murder case, surely be to good-ness, by any standards, people would realise this evidence would be put up by the Director of Public Prosecutions [DPP] to be considered by the jury.

'The reason it wasn't put up to be considered by the jury is because there was nothing to link it ultimately with Wayne O'Donoghue. Absolutely not. If there had been, it would have been put up there and we would have dealt with it, naturally. But it wasn't even at that level or standard. But it wasn't even debated in a trial within a trial context. It didn't even get to that standard of consideration.'

Mr Buttimer said the level of forensic analysis in the case was 'quite intensive', by both the State and the defence, and he said the evidence brought before the trial was: '... properly introduced. But this material didn't even merit consideration by a jury. It was not deemed evidential. That is the low standard we are dealing with here.'

When asked whether the semen allegedly found on Robert belonged to Wayne O'Donoghue, Mr Buttimer said it 'absolutely was not. If any of this forensic stuff was in any way connected with Mr O'Donoghue,' he continued, 'it would have been led in evidence before a jury.'

He acknowledged that both Wayne O'Donoghue and his defence team were taken aback by Majella Holohan's allegations. 'A copy [of the Victim Impact Statement] was furnished to the defence, to the DPP and to the court. That was done. We got a pre-prepared statement from Mrs Holohan which was a most moving statement, it was perfectly acceptable to the defence and we took no issue with it.

'What happened was that at the very tail-end of the statement, for about thirty seconds, material which was not included in the Victim Impact Statement was verbalised by Majella Holohan in a fashion that was without notice to the court, the DPP or to us. That's what happened and we are now responding to those issues.

'Victim Impact Statements are something which are not statutorily required in cases of manslaughter or murder. The judge has developed a practice – and it is a good practice in my opinion – where the bereaved are allowed to make a statement to the court to explain how the event has impacted, in this case obviously hugely, on their lives in a very, very tragic fashion. The system is that a statement will be prepared, it will be furnished to the defence, to the DPP and to the court. That was the situation yesterday.' Repeating what he had already said, he continued: 'We got a prepared statement from Mrs Holohan which was a most moving statement. It was perfectly acceptable to the defence and we took no issue with it. I think it ran to about eleven pages and it was known that she was going to read out this statement to the court. It was accepted by us and accepted by the DPP. But what happened was that, at the very tail end of it, for about thirty seconds, material which was not included in the Victim Impact Statement was verbalised by Majella Holohan in a fashion which was without notice to the Court, to the DPP and to us.

'And here we are today responding to these matters following a trial. We all feel the utmost sympathy for the Holohan family. But these things were way, way beyond anything that was evidential. In fact, most of the questions raised yesterday at the very end in that thirty-second (or so) period of time were answered within the trial context. It is just the one issue raised by her that was not evidential, the forensic matter, we take clear issue with that.'

Mr Buttimer said he understood the terrible plight facing the Holohan family, and their obvious distress at Robert's death. 'We feel the utmost sympathy for the Holohan family. I saw her [Majella] in court during the trial, I saw her yesterday and I heard her give a very humanitarian Victim Impact Statement.' But he took issue with the way his client was now being portrayed. 'Wayne is not a scurrilous person,' he said. 'Wayne is a very decent person. But it will be very difficult for him to recover from these allegations. I believe he has been very, very seriously damaged. He is a very decent, honourable young man who accepts his responsibility for the death of Robert Holohan.'

The solicitor acknowledged that the entire episode was 'a disaster' for all concerned. 'Everything, if you look at it from a certain perspective, was a disaster. You could say it was suspicious, you could say it was premeditated, you could say all these things. But what you are doing is looking into the mind of a twenty-year-old young fellow with a catastrophic event happening literally at his feet. He was in a state of trauma,' he added.

But Mr Buttimer acknowledged that he does take issue with Wayne O'Donoghue's claim to Gardaí that he often heard screams from the Holohan house – a claim described by Mrs Holohan as 'mean and nasty.' The Holohans were so upset by what O'Donoghue had told Gardaí that Majella specifically refuted it in her Victim Impact Statement. Mr Buttimer stressed that Wayne now takes no issue with Majella Holohan on this point.

But he again repeated the denial that Wayne had attempted to destroy Robert's body. 'It was just a reaction. It wasn't sinister. It wasn't a sinister thing to do in any way whatsoever. There was nothing sinister about the whole thing.

'As regards the sentence that was imposed, it was well within the bounds of sentences for manslaughter which have been reviewed by the Court of Criminal Appeal. Yesterday, it was my belief that Mr Justice Paul Carney measured the sentence completely fairly, accurately and in a balanced fashion. He gave a very reasoned delivery of a judgement as to why he was arriving at this particular sentence in regard to all of the circumstances. While people might have a certain perception, there is a lot of emotion about this case and that is perfectly understandable.

'I have also said it today that, one way or another, Wayne O'Donoghue is serving a life sentence. I stressed the importance of that to people. That is a very serious reality in the life of Wayne O'Donoghue. This sentence of imprisonment is within the bounds of fairness and reason, having regard to all of the circumstances.'

Mr Buttimer said that while Mr Justice Carney was not sentencing his client strictly for the concealment of Robert's body, it was a factor in his judgement, despite what some commentators had said.

'The judge did refer to it as an impact factor in relation to the unfortunate Holohan family. But he [Wayne] was not convicted of any crime other than manslaughter. I think he [the judge] took it into account in a certain fashion.

'The problem is this: it is a legal problem in which these things are dealt with by the prosecution and by the Gardaí. There is a rule which says that a Book of Evidence in a serious criminal case has to be made available to the accused within forty-two days [after a serious crime has been committed]. I am a criminal defence lawyer and I have always regarded it as an unsustainable situation that the prosecution has to be faced with providing a Book of Evidence, literally, and pardon the pun, with a gun held to their head, given the constraint of time. But as a general proposition, that is the law, and there is terrible pressure being put on the prosecution to put up the material so that the defence can receive it.

'And I can certainly tell you that in this particular case, while matters may have seemed to have been in a certain fashion when investigative work was carried out at the outset, when you couple that with the fact that the material has to be made available to the defence literally while investigative matters are still ongoing, you might begin to see a pattern emerging whereby something may seem to be the case at the outset, [but] at the end of the process – and these processes of a scientific nature can be extensive – it is absolutely not the case.

'The level of analysis in this case was extensive – and not, may I say, just on the prosecution side. But also on the defence side. Ultimately, what may have appeared to be something that had merited consideration at the outset, at the end of the day it was not evidential. This material did not even merit consideration by a jury. It wasn't deemed sufficiently evidential to be considered by a jury. That is the low standard. These matters were not even canvassed in court. There is no evidence to sustain these matters being put before a jury.

'These matters merited attention from January until October, and, at the end of an entire detailed consideration by the prosecution and by the defence, there was nothing which could be put before a jury which would in any way sustain any form of connection between any forensic material and Wayne O'Donoghue.'

Mr Buttimer then began to counter the various issues raised by Majella Holohan in court, ranging from her queries about Robert's mobile phone and why he was in Wayne O'Donoghue's bedroom at 7.30am.

'He wasn't [in the bedroom], and he didn't [ring him at 6.00am]. These matters were dealt with in the course of the trial. We called two witnesses as a part of our defence. The first was Professor Jack Crane who reviewed the work of Professor Marie Cassidy. The second evidence that we called was material supplied to us by the State and which we located, quite properly, on the State investigative file. It came from a worker at the premises in Midleton where Robert bought his mobile phone. It is a matter of fact, and this was considered by the jury, that Robert did not even own the telephone at the time when he was alleged, at 7.30am, to have been in Wayne O'Donoghue's house. He did not even own the phone. As a matter of proveable fact, he purchased the phone four-and-a-half hours *after* he was alleged to have been in the room. That is a fact. There is an explanation which is to do with timings and the insertion of timings into phones.

'Robert was always a very welcome guest, as always and Majella knows it, in the O'Donoghue house. He had free reign to ramble about the place. There was never any issue about that. As kids would do, he would go in there to hang out. Robert was all over Wayne's house on many, many occasions.'

In reference to Majella's claim about the 999 calls logged to Robert's phone, Mr Buttimer insisted it was simply messing around.

'There is evidence to suggest that following young Robert's purchase of the phone he rang 999. Quite frankly, he was messing on the phone – he was kidding about. He had just bought a new phone – that was the end of it. There was nothing sinister about it.'

The solicitor also stressed that the current situation was almost entirely created by what Wayne O'Donoghue did after the accidental killing of Robert, in particularly his decision to remain silent about the body's whereabouts for nine crucial days. 'We wouldn't be having this conversation if he [Wayne] had done so [contacted the Gardaí], if this thing had gone the way we hoped it would have gone yesterday in terms of explaining these matters. We had a psychiatrist in court and while psychiatry cannot explain everything, there is an explanation.

'If you had read the seven-and-a-half hour statement that Wayne made in my presence and in the presence of high-ranking members of an Garda Síochána, there is an explanation in there. But there is also a deep psychiatric explanation for a panic reaction and a reaction of digging a hole and the hole getting deeper and you cannot get out. There is this implosion of reality. Honestly, we had hoped to be able to explain these things to people yesterday and Wayne had intended to be the next witness up in the box after Majella. He did want to say these things. His father wanted to say these things. We had intended to call him. We had intended to call Dr Brian McCaffrey, a consulting psychiatrist who had dealt with Wayne since his incarceration.'

But, Mr Buttimer said, after Majella Holohan's statement there was simply no point in trying to deal with these explanations. 'The whole thrust of the matter changed once these matters were brought into the public domain. It was a matter we had to consider. But in the way things turned out, there was a high degree of emotion in the court. We had to make a decision that those intentions on our part could not be carried through.

'There was nothing sinister in this. Nothing sinister at all. This was a massive, comprehensive investigation carried out by the Gardaí.

Supt Liam Hayes said in the witness box yesterday that everything Wayne O'Donoghue said was scrutinised to the nth degree in their follow-up investigation – effectively it presented it [O'Donoghue's admission statement] as being accurate.

'The jury were able to consider the matter – they did. And over four-and-a-half hours – which, I suppose in some respects is relatively quick, because they had ten days' of material to consider – they came back with a unanimous not guilty verdict. He [Wayne] was the cause of this occurrence. But I think people should consider the ease with which this type of thing could happen. It was frightening. It was a frighteningly simple event to occur. Of course, he should have picked up the phone and rung the Gardaí or the ambulance etc. But the fact is that he didn't. He bears that burden to this day and all of the other consequences. But he was in a state of trauma.

'I hope that people kind-of understand that what we are hearing coming out yesterday is just not true, it isn't accurate in so far as it reflects in any way on Wayne. He is carrying a burden as it is. The four-year sentence is merely part of the burden, not just for Wayne, but also for his family who have had to carry this on their shoulders too. They are extremely decent people, extremely upset at all of the things that have happened up to and including events that occurred yesterday ...'

*

However, within twenty-four hours, the Holohan family had issued a statement through their solicitor, Ernest Cantillon, expressing grave concern that doubt was being cast over their statements in Ennis. Mr Cantillon, one of Cork's foremost criminal law experts, pointed out that Wayne O'Donoghue's defence team had opted not to cross-examine Majella following her Victim Impact Statement in Ennis. But now they were intent on challenging what she had said, and the solicitor said that she was deeply upset. Mr Cantillon stressed that nothing Majella said should have come as a surprise to the defence team because it was all based on material in the Garda investigation files.

'They did not avail of that [cross-examination] but yet they come out today and question the truthfulness of what she said,' he stated. 'It's not as if this is something that Majella Holohan is making up – it's truthful.

'Majella Holohan made her statement on this basis: the last person who had custody of this child was Wayne O'Donoghue. Robert had semen on his body which he did not have before. It was a natural question for her to ask: what is he doing with semen on him? She is entitled to ask that question. Why should she censor herself? I don't think it is right that she should. She must be entitled to have her say and I object to the criticism of her for doing that,' Mr Cantillon said.

Furthermore, he slated the way lofty legal aims were applied to the case with little or no consideration for the facts. 'There is a lot of palaver that it is better for a thousand people to go free rather than convict someone in the wrong. But this wasn't an innocent man. This was a man who had killed a small child. You simply do not plead guilty to causing an accident,' he said.

THE INQUEST

After two days dominating the national headlines, the story now switched direction and focused on when the coroner's inquest into Robert's death would be staged. By tradition, such inquests are never staged until all criminal proceedings are concluded. Cork (South) Coroner, Frank O'Connell, confirmed, following media inquiries, that he was going to wait until the twenty-eight-day period for possible appeals to elapse before beginning to liaise with the interested parties about when the inquest should be staged.

Having spoken to Mr O'Connell, I found two things immediately emerged: the inquest was not going to be a re-run of the trial (which is not the purpose of such hearings under the Coroner's Act) and, secondly, no details of the format of the inquest were going to be discussed until the twenty-eight-day period had expired. Until then, the coroner politely stressed that he would not be commenting on the date of the inquest and whether witnesses such as Wayne O'Donoghue or Dr Marie Cassidy would be summoned.

Under the Coroner's Act, the purpose of an inquest is to inquire into an individual's death so that key facts can be confirmed: the identity of the deceased, the location of their death and the medical cause of their death. While a trial is effectively about apportioning blame or responsibility, an inquest is strictly about confirming specific events such as the time and place of death and, ultimately, the cause of death. By law the inquest cannot attempt to apportion blame in the fashion of a quasi-trial. But a jury is required and a verdict reached. If required, coroners and their juries can add recommendations to their verdict if a safety issue or social need is perceived to be involved.

In an interview with me, Frank Buttimer stressed that his client would 'do everything humanly possible' to facilitate both the coroner and the Holohan family with the inquest. However, he said that Wayne would refuse to attend the inquest if there was any suggestion of him being subjected to an attempt at a re-trial or if he would be exposed to the type of verbal attack and accusations that had occurred in Ennis. Mr Buttimer said, in light of the purpose of an inquest, he would find it 'extraordinary' if his client were summoned to appear.

THE APPEAL

In hindsight, there shouldn't have been any surprise at the fact that Majella Holohan would write to the DPP seeking an appeal against the sentence handed down to her son's killer. But, when I confirmed at lunchtime on Friday, 27 January, that she had just posted her letter to the DPP's office, I found myself taken aback. The overwhelming consensus amongst legal experts was that the four-year term was in keeping with previous manslaughter sentences, and that Mr Justice Carney had structured his sentence and explanation, as he said himself, with one eye on the fact that the Court of Criminal Appeal had decimated many previous manslaughter sentences. What surprised me most, I suppose, was that, having endured so much, Mark and Majella Holohan were willing to suffer even further as their duty to Robert.

Majella had posted the letter to the DPP shortly before lunchtime and had then gone to her son's grave to say a prayer. More than anything, it spoke volumes about how the Holohans were determined to fight for what they saw as justice. The media, sadly, didn't make it easy for them. Despite the fact that the Holohans had built up trusted relationships with a number of Cork-based reporters and photographers, other papers felt the story had to be followed up. So the Holohans found themselves asked for quotes, interviews and photos virtually every day for the next three weeks.

Midleton Gardaí, ever mindful of the impact the case was having on the community and the two families involved, discreetly asked the media to be as sensitive as possible. When it was known that TV crews or photographers were in town for reaction from either the Holohan or O'Donoghue families, Garda liaison officers did their best to ensure that common sense prevailed.

THE ANALYSIS

After a week of exhaustive coverage of the case and the sentencing decision, the Sunday newspapers went back over everything again in great detail. But there were some interesting developments too.

One was a statement from Wayne's parents, Ray and Therese O'Donoghue. The *Sunday Tribune* printed an open letter issued by the O'Donoghues to try and address some of the sensational issues that had emerged in Ennis. The couple insisted that the death of Robert at the hands of their son, Wayne, was entirely accidental and that they were appalled at some of the media coverage that followed the hearing.

'She [Majella Holohan] raised in particular the matter of the forensic evidence. The O'Donoghue family were relieved to note that she did not in fact suggest or state that there was any link between our son and the material,' Ray O'Donoghue wrote. 'If they [the State] could have, this evidence would have been submitted in court. Therese and I, Wayne's parents, know for a fact, and Wayne has consistently confirmed, that nothing improper took place between himself and Robert. As regards Mrs Holohan's other concerns, all we can say is that these were dealt with during the trial.'

Ray O'Donoghue's letter also stated that the family were appalled by some of the media coverage which resulted from what happened in Ennis. '[The] media coverage has painted a picture so far removed from the truth that it is almost unbearable for us as a family. The O'Donoghue family wish to extend their deepest sympathy to the Holohan family on Robert's accidental death. We too mourn Rob and he is remembered daily in our prayers.' But what the letter did not reveal was that, according to Garda and legal sources, there was no contact at that time between the two families, despite Frank Buttimer, O'Donoghue's solicitor, publicly stressing that he wished there was some way to try and heal the breach between them.

The other fascinating piece was by journalist Geraldine Niland in the *Sunday Independent*. The investigative journalist had interviewed a leading British forensic psychologist, Dr Mike Berry, about the Robert Holohan case. Dr Berry, a veteran profiler who had worked with Scotland Yard and the Metropolitan Police, was consulted by Niland on the trial, the sentencing hearing and pertinent aspects of the case. His view was straightforward, and effectively endorsed the defence position.

'I don't think this crime was sexual – the evidence does not support [it] ... There are some worrying developments in the case with [the] unfair and unsupported allegations of sexual perversion,' he said. Dr Berry had worked extensively on a number of high-profile murder cases in Britain and he said he couldn't find the normal hallmarks in the Holohan case of any type of sexual motivation for the killing. It was far more likely, he said, that the boy's killing arose from a dispute or confrontation that spiralled out of hand.

Other Sunday papers went with more lurid headlines and some controversial claims about the precise scenario surrounding the DNA evidence and why it wasn't introduced during the trial. But Gardaí only reacted to one claim, emphatically denying as 'incorrect and totally without foundation' a claim that a second DNA sample had been recovered from the scene at Inch. Gardaí stressed that only one type of semen was recovered from Inch, and that, in legal terms, it was unidentified.

WEDNESDAY, 8 FEBRUARY 2006
THE UCC DEBATE

As everyone awaited the DPP's decision on whether or not to appeal the four-year jail term, attention began to focus on other issues raised by the dramatic Ennis sentencing hearing. Foremost amongst these was the whole system surrounding Victim Impact Statements. Incredibly, there is no statutory provision for these in homicide cases under Irish law, but the tradition of allowing them had emerged over recent years within the Central Criminal Court as a way of allowing victims' families an outlet for their pain, suffering and loss. But now, in the wake of Majella Holohan's dramatic eight questions and their implications, the entire future of these statements had been called into question.

Frank Buttimer was asked, during a debate organised by law students at University College Cork (UCC), to discuss his views on the system underpinning Victim Impact Statements. Not surprisingly, he had strong opinions, arguing that while Victim Impact Statements had to be retained as a vital part of the overall legal process, they needed to be provided for by legislation and, equally importantly, delivered in a controlled, regulated fashion.

'Who are we, as lawyers, operators of the legal system and judges, to tell the legislature [the Oireachtas] what the people want? Any removal of the entitlement of people as victims to have their say would be regarded as a breach of the principle that justice should be seen to be done. I am not saying that the system does not need modernisation and does not need remedial work. If the system is improved and if there is new legislation, then events of the kind that have caused some disquiet will not occur again. The message should go forth that it is a matter for the law makers and not for lawyers to deal with the problem,' Mr Buttimer said.

He added that he felt Victim Impact Statements were hugely important outlets for allowing the court to hear about the full impact of a crime, but they needed to be controlled and regulated.

MONDAY, 20 FEBRUARY 2006
THE CHALLENGE

A little more than ninety minutes before the deadline, the DPP lodged an eleventh-hour challenge to the four-year jail term. Shortly before 3.30pm, appeal documents were lodged by the State over Wayne O'Donoghue's sentence – exactly one month after an appeal from Robert's mother, Majella, to the DPP to challenge the perceived leniency of the four-year term.

The late timing of the appeal took not only legal experts and media commentators by surprise, it also shocked friends of the O'Donoghue family who had not expected the sentence to be challenged. The appeal primarily cited the undue leniency of the sentence, given the overall circumstances of the case, as well as five specific elements of the trial.

These included how Wayne O'Donoghue tried to conceal the body, how he attempted to shield his part in the boy's death, how he repeatedly attempted to frustrate the Garda investigation and the discovery of the body, as well as the major difference in size and strength between the duo and the injuries ultimately suffered by Robert.

The challenge, which was lodged under the Criminal Justice Act (1993), would be heard by the Court of Criminal Appeal, who can either refuse the application or quash the sentence and then impose a term that it considers more appropriate. The process was expected to take at least six months to conclude.

An emotional Majella Holohan said they were 'relieved and thrilled' by the DPP's decision. 'We welcome the decision made by the DPP and we would also like to express our sincere thanks to the thousands of people who have supported us over the past few weeks,' she said. The Holohans were taken aback by the thousands of cards, letters and messages of support sent to them since the controversy erupted over the four-year jail term handed down to their son's killer.

Friends stressed that the couple are very grateful for the Director's decision and do not want to jeopardise the process by further comment. 'It has been a very difficult month for them, but this news is certainly something that they were hoping for,' one family friend said. The Holohans' solicitor, Ernest Cantillon, declined to comment on the appeal or the family's next move.

By policy, the DPP does not comment on individual cases or prosecutions. But the O'Donoghue family were shocked at the sentence appeal, which was totally unexpected. They were also taken aback by the last-minute nature of the appeal. Initially, Frank Buttimer declined to comment on the appeal, stressing that he himself had only received the appeal papers in the afternoon and wanted time to consider them.

However, the following day, he confirmed what everyone already suspected: that Wayne O'Donoghue would contest the appeal and fight to serve out his original four-year jail term. 'I have no doubt they [the Court of Appeal] will treat this properly and fairly,' Mr Buttimer said. 'But they will be constrained by law to the matters which were dealt with during the hearing of the trial and the sentencing hearing.'

Mr Buttimer said that while his client was taken aback by the appeal decision, he understands that the DPP is acting within his rights. 'He accepts that there is a process. He was fully aware that there was going to be an opportunity for the DPP within the twenty-eight-day period to lodge a notice of appeal. So Wayne accepts he is going to have to undergo an appeal process now and he is prepared to deal with that. He seems to be not too bad about it and he is going to face up to it.'

However, the solicitor admitted that it is possible that the appeal may not be resolved for up to nine months. 'I do know that the Court of Criminal Appeal already has a significant number of matters before it at the moment,' he said. 'It [the appeal] certainly won't happen in the immediate future. My own estimate is on average approximately six to nine months from the time the appeal is served.'

The appeal itself, which will be heard by a three-judge panel comprised of one Supreme Court and two High Court judges, will be based on transcripts of the trial and sentencing hearing as well as legal submissions from both the State and the defence. But Mr Buttimer stressed that the Court of Appeal hearing will not be a retrial, but merely a review of sentence. 'The jury obviously accepted that this was an accidental killing and it is on that basis that Judge Carney imposed sentence on the manslaughter verdict.'

SUNDAY 30 APRIL 2006
THE PRISON INTERVIEW

After two months in which the case had gradually faded from the headlines, the controversy over the Robert Holohan killing once again re-erupted with a vengeance when Wayne O'Donoghue gave a dramatic interview from the Midlands Prison.

It was widely known that O'Donoghue was deeply unhappy about the media coverage of his sentencing hearing and the emphasis placed on Majella Holohan's DNA claims. In particular, he took objection to two elements of coverage by TV3 and the *Irish Sun* newspaper. But, despite that fact, he had declined numerous requests for interviews or comments beyond the statements made by his solicitor, Frank Buttimer, in the wake of both the Central Criminal Court trial and the Ennis sentencing.

However, the O'Donoghue family appeared to have developed a relationship with the *Sunday Tribune*, issuing a statement in the wake of the sentencing hearing solely to the Sunday paper and then, in April, agreeing to an exclusive interview with Wayne from prison. The story, written by Conor McMorrow, offered a detailed insight into Wayne O'Donoghue's reaction to the trial, his feelings about what Majella Holohan had said before the court at Ennis, his relationship with Rebecca Dennehy and his future plans. It even dealt with prison life for the young student and the suggestion that he was the focus of death-threats inside the jail.

The interview opened with Wayne apologising to the Holohan family for his actions and insisting that: 'I am not a paedophile.' He was also adamant that the traces of semen found at the scene in Inch were not his.

'I have no problem doing my time in here [Midlands Prison],' he stated, 'but there is no way there was anything going on between Robert and myself. I cannot say how sorry I am for everything that happened to them. I will feel sorry for what I did until the day I die. I never stop thinking about what happened. I think about it 24/7. I think about the Holohan family a lot, as they have lost Robert out of all this.'

The core element of the interview was the revelation of details of the defence's forensic report conducted by scientist Emma Lynch of Hayward Associates in Cambridge. It was this report which cast doubt on the State's identification of the DNA samples, and ultimately resulted in the entire DNA issue being kept out of the Central Criminal Court trial.

The Hayward report categorically denied that there was any scientific basis for supporting the view that any illicit contact took place between Wayne O'Donoghue and Robert Holohan. It put forward the explanation that any DNA samples found were probably there by accidental transfer.

'It is possible that semen was transferred to Robert Holohan's hands and nails indirectly, for example, as a result of him having been placed on the semi-stained bath mat,' Ms Lynch explained. The Hayward report indicated that, for the purposes of cross-checking, DNA samples were taken from Wayne's father, Ray, and his two brothers, Nicky and Timmy. The report indicated that the DNA samples recovered from the bath mat matched samples taken from one of Wayne's family members.

But Wayne O'Donoghue insisted in the interview that, in light of this forensic evidence, he was stunned at the claims levelled during the Ennis sentencing hearing. 'I couldn't believe it when Majella got up and said that there was semen on Robert's body during her Victim Impact Statement. That semen was definitely not mine – and I couldn't believe it when people started to say that there was anything going on between us. But I don't hold anything against her [Majella] for what she said – I can see why she came out with what she said.'

O'Donoghue again insisted that it was only out of shock that he dumped Robert's body at Inch and then kept silent about what happened while the huge search operation continued for nine days. 'I was in such a state of shock and panic throughout those days – I had not slept or anything. I can say that the night I handed myself in I had the best night's sleep I ever had in my life as I hadn't slept at all in days.'

He stressed that the only person in the world he knew he could tell was his father, and he was certain that his father would know the right thing to do. 'I just couldn't keep going on not telling anyone what had happened to Robert, so I told my father.' The statement to the Gardaí and the fact that the truth finally came out was an enormous relief, he said.

But he admitted that the aftermath of the sentencing hearing was the worst of all with the allegations of paedophilia dramatically impacting on him. In the weeks after Majella's Victim Impact Statement, a number of his friends stopped contacting him and the flow of letters of sympathy dried up. 'I can understand why they started to believe it when I was called a paedophile across the front of some of the papers,' he said. Now, Wayne O'Donoghue said he takes comfort in prayer – and stressed that faith has been an important ally for him in prison.

As to the future, Wayne O'Donoghue said that the high-profile nature of the case makes it virtually certain that his immediate future lies outside Midleton, Cork and Ireland. 'I am not really sure what I will do [on release from prison]. I take each day one at a time in here but I will probably go abroad for a few years. I might go to England or somewhere and see after that about coming back to Ireland.'

He concluded by stressing, once again, how he regrets what happened that terrible 4 January day, and how the Holohans remain in his prayers.

Not surprisingly, the *Sunday Tribune* made maximum use of their 'scoop', devoting their entire front page to the story as well as three full inside pages. For the next two days, every other newspaper, television and radio station was playing catch-up. But there was unease – particularly within the Holohan family – at the selective nature of the interview. Friends of the Holohans expressed concern at the prospect that the only detailed personal response Wayne O'Donoghue might make to the issues of concern surrounding the case could prove to be through a newspaper column – depending on what happens with the coroner's inquest.

*

The main follow-up to the story was the reaction of Mark and Majella Holohan to the comments of their son's killer. The couple once again insisted they did not want to say anything that would jeopardise the judicial process, namely the Court of Criminal Appeal hearing. 'We don't want to get [dragged] into any tit-for-tat battle,' Mark Holohan explained. But he said that it had been a very difficult fortnight for the family, particularly given the timing of the interview by Wayne O'Donoghue in the week that Robert should have received his confirmation.

As a mark of solidarity, Robert's Midleton classmates had laid flowers on his grave and messages of sympathy were passed to the Holohan family. A special shrine to Robert at Inch – which had been vandalised by thugs in mid-April – was also in the process of being re-paired. It all added up to painful reminders of their loss for the Holohans.

Majella Holohan insisted to several reporters that, despite what Wayne O'Donoghue said, she firmly stood over her sensational comments in Ennis. 'We stand over what was said. But he [Wayne] should tell the truth. That's what we want. Let him stand over what he has said. Let him go into Court and say those things. I will be there every step of the way for my son. Everything we have said is the truth,' she added, saying that she was 'deeply shocked' by the prison interview.

Not surprisingly, the interview re-ignited the entire debate over the trial and four-year sentence. Newspapers that had requests for interviews ignored predictably reacted with outrage. The Irish *Daily Mail* dismissed the interview as entirely 'self-serving', while the tabloids once again focused on what life inside the Midlands Prison was like for Wayne O'Donoghue. In particular, they focused on the revelation that Wayne O'Donoghue insisted he had friends inside the prison and that in the prison garden he would often meet Padraig Nally, the Mayo farmer jailed for having shot and killed a trespasser on his farm.

Unable to interview O'Donoghue, several tabloids focused their attention on Rebecca Dennehy, and, within weeks of the O'Donoghue interview, carried stories and photos that the young Midleton girl was now seeing someone else.

FRIDAY 12 MAY 2006
THE DEFAMATION ACTION

The dust from Wayne O'Donoghue's sensational prison interview had hardly begun to settle when the case took another twist, this time with the confirmation that High Court papers had been served on behalf of O'Donoghue alleging defamation against two media outlets, TV3 and the *Irish Sun*. Both had been the focus of complaints from Wayne O'Donoghue in the aftermath of the Ennis sentencing hearing, and O'Donoghue's solicitor, Frank Buttimer, had written to both in the weeks following. Now, Wayne O'Donoghue was suing them for libel and papers were lodged in the High Court.

Once again, Mark and Majella Holohan stated that they were shocked by the development. While the couple declined to comment further, a family friend felt that they would likely 'look favourably' on any request from the media organisations, as part of any defence of the action, for them to give direct evidence. Another family source said that if they were requested to offer evidence in defence of any defamation action, it was likely that they would be favourably disposed towards it. The family would take a close interest in any action that would result in some of their questions being put directly to Wayne O'Donoghue.

MONDAY, 22 MAY 2006
THE APPEAL DATE

In a brief hearing, the Court of Criminal Appeal confirmed that it would hear the DPP's case against the leniency of Wayne

O'Donoghue's four-year prison sentence on 13 July 2006, but this was later moved to 27 July. On 27 July the Court reserved its judgement and it is expected that it will publish it in October. The three-judge panel will make its decision based entirely on trial and sentencing transcripts, coupled with detailed submissions from the prosecution and defence in relation to the core issues. The coroner's inquest into Robert's death will be staged a minimum of one month after their ruling.

CHAPTER 14: THE EIGHT QUESTIONS

The chasm between what Wayne O'Donoghue insisted was a tragic accident and the Holohan family's belief that serious questions remained unanswered revolved around eight key issues. Those queries, raised by Majella Holohan, were at the heart of the conflicting positions of the O'Donoghue and Holohan legal teams.

On the one hand, Frank Buttimer insisted that all the relevant matters had been adequately and fully dealt with during the ten-day Central Criminal Court trial. The forensic matter – that of the semen found on Robert's hand – he dismissed as having absolutely no link to his client. Quite properly, he insisted, the material was not even submitted for consideration during the trial. However, Ernest Cantillon, for the Holohans, stressed that, far from being dealt with, the issues raised by Majella Holohan still remained to be fully and properly explained after the trial.

QUESTION ONE: Why was semen found on Robert's body?
Wayne O'Donoghue's legal team insist that the DNA material involved is in no way whatsoever linked to him. There was no definitive idea as to who the DNA sample belonged to.

The decision not to introduce that material during the trial rested entirely with the prosecution. There was no legal argument of its admission and Mr Justice Paul Carney was not asked to consider its admissibility. As far as the jury were concerned, it never existed.

O'Donoghue's defence team stressed that it was not their responsibility to go further than this. Proving who the semen belonged to was entirely an issue for the State. 'The reason it [the DNA] wasn't put up to be considered by the jury is because there was nothing to link it ultimately with Wayne O'Donoghue. But it wasn't even debated within a trial context. It didn't even get to that standard of consideration. That is the low standard that was involved,' Frank Buttimer said.

As part of Wayne O'Donoghue's Midlands Prison interview it was revealed that the DNA sample recovered from the bath mat in the O'Donoghue's home matched samples taken from one of Wayne's family members. All three male members of the O'Donoghue household had supplied DNA samples for cross-referencing purposes. O'Donoghue's legal team are adamant that accidental cross-contamination occurred when Robert's hand was lying on the mat and this explains the DNA traces subsequently found at Inch. Wayne O'Donoghue is adamant that the DNA sample found was not his.

QUESTION TWO: Why was Robert in Wayne's bedroom at 7.30am in the morning?

Wayne O'Donoghue insists, again through his legal team, that this question arose from a simple misunderstanding during the trial. Robert's silver Nokia 3200 phone indicated that a snap of a poster on Wayne's bedroom wall was taken at 7.30am on 28 December. But the phone was set to the incorrect time period, and Robert did not own the phone at this time.

'He [Robert] was not in the bedroom at that time. It was an issue due to [phone] timings. He [Robert] didn't even own the phone at the time he was alleged to have been in Wayne's bedroom,' Frank Buttimer explained. Robert, in fact, had bought the phone at Xtra-vision shortly before 12.00 noon that day. The clear suggestion is that the picture was taken at 7.30pm on the evening of 28 December.

QUESTION THREE: Why did Robert make two 999 calls in the eight days before his death?

Majella Holohan's revelation in her Victim Impact Statement about the two 999 emergency calls made by Robert in the days after he bought the new Nokia phone brought a swift response from Wayne O'Donoghue's legal team. In one radio interview Frank Buttimer said that Robert was simply playing around with the handset: 'Quite frankly, he [Robert] was messing about. He was just kidding about. He had just bought the phone. There was nothing sinister about it. No adverse inference could be drawn from it.' He said that Robert had just purchased the new camera phone and was merely showing it off to an audience, ringing whatever numbers came into his head, as youngsters do.

Not long after these questions were raised it emerged that the Gardaí had traced and examined the logs for both calls. In each case, the caller never spoke and immediately disconnected the line once the 999 emergency operator spoke. In both cases, the calls lasted a mere matter of seconds. Gardaí simply had no reason to trace the 999 calls at the time.

QUESTION FOUR: Why didn't Wayne O'Donoghue tell someone what happened?

The defence offer panic and trauma as the obvious explanations. Frank Buttimer pointed out that there was a clear psychological explanation for the young man's failure to own up until after the body had been found, and stated that this explanation would have been offered in Ennis but for the dramatic eight questions levelled by Majella Holohan. O'Donoghue's initial plan to commit suicide was put aside and, as the search escalated for Robert, Wayne was simply unable to confront the enormity of what he had done.

Buttimer also denied that there was anything sinister about Wayne O'Donoghue's actions between 4 and 15 January – while acknowledging that, had he contacted either the Gardaí or told his family, 'We wouldn't be where we are today.'

But for the Holohans, panic and trauma simply don't explain away the many curious aspects of Wayne O'Donoghue's behaviour over those nine terrible days. Why offer to ring Robert's mobile phone in front of Robert's mother knowing it was just hours after he'd killed the boy? Why take part in the search effort for six days and, on one occasion, make a point of angrily confronting two Gardaí over the decision to scale-back the search operation on safety grounds?

The Holohans believe that Wayne O'Donoghue's actions were nothing but cool and calculating over those nine days, particularly in the hours immediately after Robert's death. He placed Robert's bike to make it appear that the boy had been abducted. He took time to clean his house to make sure there was no trace of Robert having been there. He even stopped – *en route* to dump the boy's body – to buy a bottle of Lucozade. He called to see his girlfriend, Rebecca, and consciously tried to act normal. Just four hours after he had killed Robert, Wayne O'Donoghue took his family dog for a walk, played PlayStation games with his girlfriend, remembered to return a DVD to Xtra-vision and then spent part of the evening watching television with Rebecca in her house.

He was even conscious enough to go back to Inch and try to destroy the plastic bags around the boy's body – while denying he was attempting to damage the remains. And both search volunteers and Gardaí commented on the fact that he was extremely interested in crucial aspects of the search operation – the locations being examined by volunteers and whether tracking dogs could follow a scent from vehicles. In one Garda statement, given just days after Robert's death, Wayne O'Donoghue clearly tried to infer that something strange was going on in the Holohan home, claiming he heard screams there.

Wayne O'Donoghue never offered the Gardaí any clue, not even an anonymous phone call, about where Robert's remains might be found. And the timing of his first statement of admission was pointed: it was just minutes after he had read in the Sunday newspapers of 16 January that Gardaí had recovered fingerprints from the plastic wrappings found around the body at Inch strand. As part of the Garda 'elimination sample' procedure, O'Donoghue had offered fingerprints along with other people in the Midleton area on 14 January, the day before Robert was buried.

QUESTION FIVE: Why were both of Robert's runners off when his body was found if he was about to cycle away from the O'Donoghue home?

To many people who read the Ennis Victim Impact Statement, this was one of the most curious aspects of what Majella Holohan said. But, if you sat through the ten-day Central Criminal Court trial, this question took on added significance. Majella told the trial that Robert informed her he was asked to take off his shoes while in the O'Donoghue home, largely to protect the floor coverings. Wayne O'Donoghue insisted that the fatal confrontation with Robert occurred *outside* his house, on the gravel driveway by his Fiat car. The confrontation occurred, he added, as Robert was preparing to cycle away.

Mr Buttimer said that the evidence during the trial clearly indicated that, after the fatal confrontation outside the O'Donoghue home, Wayne brought Robert's limp body inside to the bungalow's bathroom. The Central Criminal Court trial heard that, during this process, one of Robert's shoes came off. Wayne O'Donoghue placed the runner inside a black plastic rubbish bag with the body, which he dumped at Inch strand, some twelve miles away.

But Shane Murphy SC, for the State, laid great emphasis in his case summary on the fact that Robert's body was discovered with *both* shoes off – and one of those Nike runners had a plastic bag shoved up into its toe. Majella Holohan suggested that while one runner might come off, the fact that both were off her son's feet was a significant issue – particularly when her son, who was a very active boy, had been cycling and playing football all morning; presumably, the shoes were on his feet in a firm fashion so that they would not come off during such energetic pursuits. She claimed this fact impacts on when and how Robert went into the O'Donoghue home.

But in his prison interview Wayne O'Donoghue offered a further scenario for how Robert's second runner might have fallen off. He claimed that the first shoe came off while he was dragging the boy's body from the driveway into his home. Now, he believes that the second runner could have come off while the body was in the boot of his car.

'When I got to Inch, his other shoe had come off. I was in such a state [of shock] at the time that I must have been driving around the back roads to Inch at about a hundred miles per hour. The body would have been thrown about in the boot and that could be how the other shoe came off,' he said.

QUESTION SIX: Why weren't there any stone 'chips' found on the paintwork of Wayne O'Donoghue's car to verify his story that Robert had been throwing stones at it?

The trial heard that Robert 'popped' gravel at the side of the gold-coloured car. But a Garda forensic expert told the trial that, despite a detailed analysis of the vehicle, no trace of stone chips or flakes from the paintwork could be found that would indicate the vehicle was being targeted.

But Wayne O'Donoghue's defence team pointed out that it was never stated these stones were thrown with great force, making it likely that such small stones would not leave a mark or 'chip' on the paintwork. The defence further stressed that the overall version of events offered by Wayne O'Donoghue to Gardaí on the evening of 16 January 2005 was confirmed in all major details by their subsequent investigation and analysis. The defence said that this was conceded during the trial process by both the Gardaí and, crucially, by the State Pathologist, Dr Marie Cassidy.

However, for the Holohans it is a question of a statement without forensic or tangible evidence to support it – and the only person who could contradict him, Robert, is dead. Majella Holohan is unhappy with the 'stone throwing' as an explanation for what provoked the fatal row. Would anyone, she asked, get involved in a confrontation that would cost an eleven-year- old boy his life over something as simple as throwing stones?

QUESTION SEVEN: Why were images found to have been deleted from Robert's mobile phone and why was the phone itself free of fingerprints?

Until Majella's Victim Impact Statement, the only emphasis on Robert's mobile phone had been its crucial role in the successful location of his body at Inch. But Majella raised the issue of why fingerprints were not found on the handset and why images were deleted from the phone memory. The Gardaí knew that Robert was using the phone before his death and, during the search operation, they confirmed that the boy had been making phone calls on the handset until he had run out of credit.

Until Majella's comments in Ennis, it was not known that fingerprints had not been found on the phone or that images may have been deleted from its memory. The picture remaining – that of a joke student poster – was taken in Wayne O'Donoghue's bedroom. But no evidence was offered during the trial about the phone's memory or the issue of fingerprints not being found on the handset when it was recovered in Robert's tracksuit pocket at Inch.

Garda fingerprint evidence was offered as regards the plastic bags found at the scene at Inch but there was no reference whatsoever during the trial to the mobile phone.

The response of Wayne O'Donoghue's defence team reverts back to the phone's setting and timings and the confusion that the incorrect setting caused. The defence are adamant that there is nothing sinister involved. Furthermore, the defence were prepared to call evidence during the trial, had it been required, that the poster snapshot had been taken by Robert and not by Wayne.

QUESTION EIGHT: Why were Wayne and Robert talking on the phone at 6.00am?

Majella again raised a question which reflected on the precise nature of the relationship between Robert and Wayne O'Donoghue. She asked why any twenty-year-old would want to talk to an eleven-year-old at that hour of the morning? This query directly reflects what an examination of Robert's mobile phone handset indicated.

However, the defence insisted that these calls simply did not happen in the manner suggested and, while Robert may again have been messing around with his mobile phone, no conversations took place between the two at this hour of the morning.

Importantly, the trial was not asked to consider any evidence on what calls were made or received on Robert's mobile. The only testimony offered by the State on Robert's mobile came via an O_2 engineer who explained how the signal was traced so that search teams could be given a specific area to examine for the boy's remains. The breakdown of the calls made on the Nokia handset in the eight days that Robert owned the phone was never placed before the jury.

However, O'Donoghue's defence team also studied detailed billing records from both O_2 and Vodafone – the mobile phone suppliers to Wayne O'Donoghue and Robert Holohan – and found no evidence of any communication between the duo at any time between 6.00am and 7.00am.

APPENDIX I: THE CORONER'S INQUEST

TUESDAY, 12 SEPTEMBER 2006

The decision to open the coroner's inquest into Robert Holohan's death before the Court of Criminal Appeal returned their verdict took many by surprise. But it quickly emerged that while identification and medical evidence would be heard, the inquest would then be adjourned on the application of the Gardaí. It remained unclear whether the inquest would ever be re-opened.

In the event, only two witnesses gave evidence before Cork (South) Coroner, Frank O'Connell, at the inquest in Midleton Courthouse. These were Det. Sgt Brian Goulding, one of the senior investigating officers, and the State Pathologist, Dr Marie Cassidy. The inquest was delayed from 11.00am until 2.00pm and then lasted a total of ninety minutes – with the most dramatic events surrounding the personal cross-examination conducted by Mark and Majella Holohan. The handful of witnesses, family, Gardaí and onlookers, were dwarfed by a huge media presence as Robert's death once again dominated the national headlines.

It immediately became apparent that the coroner would not permit Mark Holohan to question the Garda witness on the issue of motive in his son's death. Mark opened the cross-examination by asking Det. Sgt Goulding: 'Do you think there was a sexual motive in the killing of

Robert Holohan?' The coroner immediately intervened and warned that he could not allow such a question.

'I cannot allow that question today – I am not saying you will not be able to find that out or pursue it. But for today we are concerning our-selves with the cause of death,' Mr O'Connell said, stressing that he understood the question was important to the Holohan family. But Mark Holohan insisted that the question and its answer were crucial. 'Surely me and my family have the right to ask that question,' he said. Mr O'Connell explained that once the inquest was adjourned he would consider any such submissions from the family.

After Dr Cassidy gave her detailed medical evidence on the cause of Robert's death – effectively reviewing the testimony she gave to the Central Criminal Court – Majella began an intensive cross-examination of the pathologist. The Holohans eventually lodged a total of nineteen questions to the pathologist – and dramatically put an alter-native version of their son's death to Dr Cassidy.

It emerged that Mark and Majella were consulting with legal and forensic experts to piece together their son's last moments – and offer an alternative version of his death to that given by Wayne O'Donoghue.

'[Could it be] that Robert was grabbed by the arm, thrown onto the ground hitting his head, he [the accused] sat on him and then strangled him? Could that have happened?' Majella asked the pathologist. Dr Cassidy said that such a version would be consistent with the bruises she found on Robert's body. 'I cannot say that that didn't happen,' the pathologist said. Crucially, the Holohans believe that this version of Robert's death fully accounts for all of the bruises and injuries to his body, including inexplicable bruises found on the boy's scalp.

The thirty-minute cross-examination of Dr Cassidy conducted by Majella, which was marked by Majella's remarkable composure, politeness and efficiency, focused on the injuries sustained by Robert, specifically the bruises to his scalp, mouth, neck and chest. In one emotional question, Majella said the family wanted to know the precise details of how Robert died. 'How long did Wayne O'Donoghue strangle my little boy? How long did my little boy suffer?' she asked.

Dr Cassidy explained that she could not say for certain how long Robert suffered, but she said the young boy would not have endured any pain, stressing that he most likely slipped into unconsciousness quite quickly.

Once the Holohans had concluded their cross-examination of Dr Cassidy, Chief Supt Liam Hayes applied under Section 25 (2) of the Coroner's Act for the inquest to be adjourned until all criminal proceedings were concluded. Mr O'Connell agreed to the application and said he would leave the adjournment date open.

Leabharlanna Poibli Chathair Baile Átha Cliath
Dublin City Public Libraries

APPENDIX II

ROBERT HOLOHAN: Robert Holohan was born on 30 June 1993. He was six months shy of his twelfth birthday when he died. Robert is buried in the family plot behind Midleton's Church of the Holy Rosary. His grave is noticeable from the number of flowers and tributes that are regularly left by family and friends. Midleton CBS, Robert's former school, has commemorated his memory through a special tree which was planted in the boy's name. The spot where his body was discovered at Inch strand is marked by a simple wooden cross. In time, it is hoped to erect a more permanent memorial. On 29 March, just two months after the Ennis sentencing hearing, the Holohan family were shocked when Gardaí informed them that the shrine to Robert's memory at Inch had been vandalised. The cross was torn from the ground and toys and memorabilia left by Robert's friends and schoolmates were scattered all over the surrounding ditches and fields.

MARK, MAJELLA, EMMA AND HARRY HOLOHAN: The family are still awaiting that most difficult of processes for the victims of violent crime – closure. They are currently considering the sale of their beautiful dormer bungalow and two acres of landscaped gardens at Ballyedmond. Understandably, the couple feel there are just too many painful memories around the area for them to be able to offer their other children a normal life there. Every time they look out their door, they see the place where Robert died.

Worse still, every time Mark and Majella drive their children to school in Midleton, they pass the spot where Robert's bike was dumped. It seems that everything in Ballyedmond is a reminder of Robert. But while no formal offers for the house have been considered as yet, they do expect to sell and move to another part of Midleton. The couple have already looked at several potential estates and sites.

Harry and Emma are both getting on well, though they still talk about Robert. Both children have attended counselling and, all things considered, are doing as well as can be expected. But they have the huge advantage of having such loving parents. Majella still works in the home while Mark's construction business continues to thrive.

The couple are awaiting the outcome of the DPP's challenge to the leniency of Wayne O'Donoghue's four-year jail term. Once that is concluded, the only formal process still outstanding is the inquest into their son's death. This will happen at least one month after the Court of Criminal Appeal make their ruling. It is expected that the inquest will be staged in Midleton. Majella has declined all requests for interviews until after the legal process is formally concluded.

WAYNE O'DONOGHUE: The former CIT student is not expected to know until early autumn 2006 the outcome of the DPP's challenge in the Court of Criminal Appeal to the alleged leniency of his four-year jail sentence for Robert Holohan's manslaughter. The Court appeal was scheduled for 27 July, six months after the Ennis sentencing hearing.

If his sentence is not increased, he can expect to qualify for remission for good behaviour while in prison, which will cut one year off his four-year term. Also, allowing for the fact that he had not sought bail and has been in custody since 16 January 2005 when he made his first admission of involvement in Robert's death, his sentence effectively started from that date. Depending on a number of factors, he can expect to finish his sentence sometime between September 2007 and January 2008. Wayne, who was born on Hallowe'en 1984, is likely to be twenty-three years old when he is released.

His family have repeatedly declined to comment about his future plans once he is released from prison. But his friends have privately said that they think Wayne will emigrate. As one friend told me: 'Wayne is just too well known here. It would be just too hard to start rebuilding his life here with all the recognition and memories.' However, he is understood to be keen to try to resume his engineering studies, probably overseas. O'Donoghue himself said that his immediate future, on release from prison, almost certainly rested outside Ireland.

He has been studying while in prison, though he has also had a number of medical problems to contend with.

Both his family and friends remain worried as to his mental and emotional state, given the trauma of the sentencing hearing and various threats directed at him from other inmates while in prison.

In early May 2006 papers were served at the High Court on Wayne O'Donoghue's behalf alleging that he had been defamed by reports on both TV3 and the *Irish Sun* newspaper. The papers were lodged by O'Donoghue's solicitor, Frank Buttimer, who declined to comment further on the matter. To date, no newspaper or broadcaster has published an apology in relation to the coverage of the sentencing hearing. If the action proceeds to a hearing it could take up to two years to secure a court date.

RAY, THERESE, NICKY AND TIMMY O'DONOGHUE: The O'Donoghue family have not lived at their Ballyedmond home since 16 January 2005. Except for a brief period, when the house was rented by a couple working in Cork, the house has lain empty. Friends say that the family are unlikely ever to return to the house where they lived so happily since the early 1980s. It is expected it will be sold once all the Court proceedings are concluded.

The family are currently staying in a rented premises in another part of East Cork. Their two other sons, Nicky and Timmy, are proceeding with their studies. Both plan to pursue third-level studies in Ireland. Ray and Therese regularly visit Wayne in the Midlands Prison. The couple have stressed that they include Robert Holohan in all their prayers and that they sympathise with the Holohan's tragic loss.

Ray continues to run his car-sales business in Cobh, some ten miles from Midleton. The family have repeatedly declined to comment to the media on the trial or Majella Holohan's Victim Impact Statement questions.

REBECCA DENNEHY: She sat her Leaving Certificate in Midleton the summer following Wayne's arrest before opting to take up third-level studies in Cork Institute of Technology, the same college where Wayne had been studying. However, she then opted to take a break from her studies and travelled to the UK.

She remains in contact with Wayne O'Donoghue and his family. She has repeatedly refused all requests for comment or interviews from the media. In the weeks following the sentencing hearing, she refused substantial cash offers from several British-owned newspapers to sell her story or provide pictures of herself and Wayne.

By May 2006 Rebecca Dennehy's relationship with Wayne O'Donoghue seemed to have become one of friendship. In his prison interview with the *Sunday Tribune*, O'Donoghue insisted that the couple were still an item, but several tabloid newspapers reported in the weeks following that Rebecca was now seeing someone else.

SUPT LIAM HAYES: Within weeks of the Holohan case being resolved, Liam Hayes was promoted to Chief Superintendent. A respected member of An Garda Síochána, his promotion came as little surprise. He is still awaiting final assignment for his new position. He remains in close contact with the Holohan family, who readily say that he was one of those most responsible for helping them through the ordeal of the trial and sentencing hearing.

FR BILLY O'DONOVAN: Just weeks after Robert's funeral, the Midleton curate was promoted to parish priest and re-assigned outside Midleton. While parishioners were delighted at his promotion, they were also sorry to see the popular priest leave the Midleton parish. However, Fr O'Donovan remains a frequent visitor to the East Cork town and was specifically asked to say Robert Holohan's first anniversary Mass by his parents.

COMMANDANT DAN HARVEY: The man who played a major role in co-ordinating the Defence Forces' support of the search effort for Robert Holohan is currently completing an advanced training course at the Curragh Camp. He is then expected to return to his normal post at the Southern Brigade headquarters in Collins Barracks, Cork. A respected author and historian, as well as a veteran of UN missions in the Lebanon, he continues to write articles of military interest.

FRANK BUTTIMER: The solicitor continues to run one of the busiest and most successful law practices in Cork. He remains involved in a number of high-profile criminal and civil cases as well as the ongoing appeal process over Wayne O'Donoghue's four-year sentence. He has already vowed that his client will 'do everything humanly possible' to assist the coroner when Robert's inquest is finally staged. Amongst Frank Buttimer's other high-profile cases is the High Court appeal by Ian Bailey over his sensational Cork Circuit Civil Court libel case involving six Irish and British newspapers over material arising from the coverage of the Sophie Toscan du Plantier murder investigation.

ERNEST CANTILLON: Like Frank Buttimer, he continues to run one of the busiest law practices in Cork. He will handle the coroner's inquest for the Holohan family when it is finally staged.

ASSISTANT COMMISSIONER TONY HICKEY: Now retired, the Robert Holohan case was one of his last major investigations as boss of the National Bureau of Criminal Investigations (NBCI). His tenure at the NBCI is widely regarded as very significant and he remains one of the most respected detectives to have served over the past thirty years. He has remained in contact with the Holohan family and attended Robert's first anniversary Mass. Because of the time-delay involved in many criminal cases reaching the courts, he is expected to be attending trials for some time to come, despite his retirement.

CHIEF SUPT KIERAN McGANN: Within weeks of Robert Holohan's body being found, he was promoted to head the Garda Training College at Templemore, County Tipperary. He is eventually expected to return to Cork – where he has spent the bulk of his career – in a senior command role.

INSPECTOR MARTIN DORNEY: He remains stationed in Midleton and is expected, in the near future, to be earmarked for promotion.

BISHOP JOHN MAGEE: His impassioned appeal for Robert's killer to come forward marked the start of a dramatic year for the veteran cleric. Later that year, Pope John Paul II died and Bishop Magee was one of those personally invited to attend the Requiem Mass having previously served the Polish Pontiff as private secretary.

MR JUSTICE PAUL CARNEY: He remains Ireland's longest-serving judge on the Central Criminal Court. Invariably, when delivering his sentences, he refers to the role of the Court of Criminal Appeal. Under his tenure, the Central Criminal Court has continued its recent policy of staging major trials close to the areas involved, with the Court having sat in Cork, Limerick, Waterford and Mayo.

Interestingly, Mr Justice Carney delivered a paper at the National

University of Ireland at Galway in 2002 at which he examined the potential merging of the charges of murder and manslaughter under the Irish judicial system. This would involve the trial judge being allowed full discretion as to the sentence imposed. He considered that such a move would reduce the caseload facing the Central Criminal Court, would decrease the number of cases going to trial, would offer significant savings to the State and, most importantly, would spare victims the 'disappointment and trauma of a manslaughter-only verdict.'

That paper also pointed out that the Central Criminal Court faced fifty-five murder cases in 2002 compared to just twenty-five in 1996. Mr Justice Carney said it was fascinating that, of the cases dealt with that year, there was not a single outright acquittal for murder. The issue in contention was manslaughter or unintentional killing as compared to murder.

JUDGE MICHAEL PATTWELL: He remains on the East Cork District Court area. He continues to expound forthright views on the criminal justice system, ranging from the use of suspended sentences to the introduction of electronic tagging of prisoners on early release.

Bibliography

Baden, Dr Michael & Roach, Marion, *Dead Reckoning*, London (Arrow Books, 2001)

CAG, *History of Cork Art*, Cork (Crawford, 1999)

Collins, Liam, *Crimes of Passion*, Dublin (Mentor Press, 2005)

Geberth, Vernon, *Homicide Investigation*, New York (CRC Press, 1996)

Harvey, Dan, and White, Gerry, *History of Victoria/Collins Barracks*, Cork (Mercier Press, 1997)

Murray, Jim, *Irish Whiskey History*, London (Trafalgar Publishing, 1997)

O'Connor, Niamh, *Cracking Crime*, Dublin (The O'Brien Press, 2002)

List of sources

Newspapers: the *Irish Independent, Sunday Independent, Evening Herald, Sunday Tribune, The Irish Times, The Star, Irish Mirror, Irish Sun, Irish Examiner, Evening Echo, Imokilly People, Sunday World, Daily Telegraph* and (London) *Independent*.

Broadcast: RTÉ, TV3, TNG, BBC Northern Ireland, BBC Radio Foyle, County Sound, 96FM, Red FM and Today FM.

Internet: Crime Scene Investigation, Katherine Ramsland; Guide to East Cork, Cork Kerry Tourism; Midleton and Jameson distillery, IDL; Law lectures, NUI Galway.

OTHER BOOKS FROM THE O'BRIEN PRESS

FATAL JOURNEY

The Murder of Trevor O'Keeffe

Eroline O'Keeffe with Jane Kelly

Eroline O'Keeffe's nightmare began in August 1987 when her son Trevor was murdered in France. It was also the beginning of her sixteen-year quest to bring his murderer – a serial killer – to justice, overcoming deliberate obstruction, judicial bungling and language barriers. An extraordinary story of love, dedication and heroic determination.

DEATH IN DECEMBER
The Story of Sophie Toscan du Plantier
Michael Sheridan

On 23 December 1996, the body of Sophie Toscan du Plantier was discovered outside her remote holiday cottage near Schull in West Cork. The murder caused shock waves in her native France and in the quiet Cork countryside that she had chosen as her retreat from the film business in which she and her husband mixed. Despite an extensive investigation, the killer is still at large. Seven years after Sophie's brutal death, an extraordinary libel hearing revealed new details of the events surrounding the murder; journalist Ralph Riegel gives a day-by-day account of what one barrister described as 'the Irish libel case of the century'.

LIFE SENTENCE

Murder Victims and their Familes

Catherine Cleary

Death in any circumstances is devastating, but when the cause is murder, grief takes on an extra dimension. Those left behind live under a life sentence, condemened to years of painful memories and deep regrets. Based on personal interviews with victims' families, Catherine Cleary tells the horrific stories of twelve murders and how their families survived the ordeal.

HOSTAGE

Notorious Irish Kidnappings

Paul Howard

When bank jobs became too risky and art heists came to nothing, the IRA hit on a simpler and more profitable way of making money: kidnapping. Pick the right target, assemble the right team and it was like winning the Lotto. Except that it didn't work out that way.

Hostage reveals the stories behind the abductions.

Send for our full-colour catalogue